MW00805772

THE HISTORICAL ORIGIN

OF

ISLAM

Islam and Christianity – Cut From the Same Cloth

Cover Design By
Walter and Arnetta Williams

Cover Compilation By
Borel Graphics, Chicago

Back Cover Photo By
Arthur Brown

Copyright©2001 by MAATHIAN PRESS, INC.
P.O. BOX 377655
CHICAGO, ILLINOIS 60637
U.S.A.

Ninth Printing, June 2020
All rights reserved. No part of this book may be
reproduced in any form or by any means without
permission in writing from the publisher.

Library of Congress
Catalog Card Number TXu 997-129
ISBN: 978-1-881040-51-4
Printed in the United States of America

THE

HISTORICAL

ORIGIN

OF

ISLAM

Islam and Christianity – Cut From the Same Cloth

By

Walter Williams

MAATHIAN PRESS, INC.
P.O. BOX 377655
CHICAGO, ILLINOIS 60637
U.S.A.

To the Memory of My Mother

LOUISE MARGARET BURCH KIMBROUGH

DEDICATION

I dedicate this book to my wife Arnetta, for without her love, devotion to me, and unrelenting love for our African Ancestors, the Ancient Egyptians, this book would have been longer coming than it has been. It was with her keen knowledge of Ancient History, World History, and her knowledge and insight concerning the three major western religions and their related literature that she was able to assist me in the research of this book. She has spent countless hours and days sitting in front of the computer, editing, and reading each chapter until we thought it ready for publication. Along with all of this, she made a profound historical contribution to this book by researching and writing an informative chapter entitled "What Happened to the Hagia Sophia.?" So to her I say thank you, thank you, thank you.

ILLUSTRATIONS

PREFACE

Religion has shaped the way the majority perceives life in their world of reality. The influence of religion also can be seen in the social, political, and economic fields of our society. In this book you will clearly see how man created a religion and a God. These pages will provide the reader factual data with regard to when man formulated the tenets of Islam and the origin of its followers.

Let us read and study through Walter Williams' collected data for a breath of fresh air. The kind of air that is full of new information that provides the African people living in America and throughout the world with new scholarship; not air that is polluted by European Theologians, Historians, or Scholars. Understanding the information written in this book or in Professor Williams' first book, "The Historical Origin of Christianity" will free you of the religious genocide that controls and directs your personal human spirituality.

By accepting a religion this causes the individual to be controlled, thereby turning the human being into a religious slave. Carter G. Woodson said it best in his book, *The Mis-Education of the Negro.* If you can control a man's thinking you do not have to worry about his actions." Africa is where the origins of Christianity, Monophysite/Muhammedanism, and Islam got its beginning. And, where Judaism, hundreds of years later created a pseudo claim for its religion.

Concerning these man-made religions, this book also holds the possibility of freeing the African mind from religious bondage. People of African decent maintain a spiritual inheritance that can overcome the shackles of a repressed mind and body. Understanding the message written in this book can begin that process. You are now armed with the weapon of research provided for you throughout these pages that can be used as a vehicle to spread the word to all Africans, especially our children. The understanding of the true origin of Christianity, Muhammedanism/Islam, and Judaism is vitally needed in the African community throughout the world in order to liberate us from these man-created religions thus stopping our spiritual destruction. This history was unknown until Walter Williams with his research, hard work, and courage put it into print. How many of us kneel and pray to an image that we know nothing about i.e., the image Jesus, the Christ, who is traditionally portrayed as a European. We only know what we have been taught by Europeans and their agents, the preachers. This type of indoctrination and ignorance only benefit and serve the European oppressors and enslavers. Perhaps, we may begin to realize why freedom is so long in coming. When we do, we will begin to rebuild our own institutions using the foundation of our great African ancestors the Ancient Egyptians as our guide. At this point we will control the education of our children, and not allow the educational system to teach them their non-African curriculum. I am certain that this book will start "born with a religion." What you were born with is an indwelling divine spiritual birthright, which is your indwelling life, spirit, or spirituality. The Creator/Creatress that used your mother and father as human instruments to bring you into this world gave this to you free at the time of your birth. Thereby, giving you a free spirituality or free spirit that dwells inside of you at this very moment. Your free spirituality that your Creator/Creatress gave you at the time of your birth is connected to and spiritually in tune with the spiritual consciousness and rhythm of the universe through your pineal gland brain fibers and your nostrils taking in the air that you breathe. One has to realize that all religions teach the believer to believe in a mythical god. And, in so doing, the Believer injects his or her free-Creator/Creatress given spirituality and spiritual power into this man created god, thereby, keeping these myths alive. When the unsuspecting believer begins to realize that GOD is a man, created by man, in man's own image and not the reverse, the reader will then understand why when speaking or using the word or term god, god always is referred to as a "he." Therefore, god has no spiritual power as god, only the spiritual powers that you, the believer, give it. I was told a profound truth when my wife, Arnetta, who said to me one day that, "god is an abstract idea that needs human spirituality to give it life." Whether one calls god Christ, Allah, Yahweh (Jehovah), or Buddha, all are man made and can only be used for religious purposes. Outside of religion god has no power.

Religion and religious literature through Western institutions are controlling the world masses via churches, mosques, synagogues, the news media, and the organized academic system. This is enforced by the powers that control the world politically, militarily and economically. You must further realize that you were not born with a religion of any kind. Man gave you a religion and God, not your Creator/Creatress. Your Creator/Creatress provided for you everything needed for you to spiritually sustain yourself for a lifetime. By not understanding your natural spiritual connection with the Universe, you allow man to confuse and substitute your natural given spiritual birthright with one of his man-created unnatural religions.

As this information is examined, it will also lead persons in the African Diaspora to understand why they must escape the bondage and the destruction of Islam and all other man-made religions, such as Christianity, Judaism, Black Hebrewism, Buddhism, etc. They must learn of our African ancestors' spiritual way of life, particularly the Ancient Egyptians. We must resurrect Ancient Egypt into our consciousness. And, we must share with our children the greatness of their ancestors, the Ancient Egyptians who are Africans, and learn of the spiritual connection they had with the universe and the Creator/Creatress as detailed in Chapter I. With this knowledge and understanding, you will begin to find your way back to your own Creator/Creatress given spirituality and your indwelling spiritual power that's connected to the universe. The information written in this book is very vital to our African community at this time in world history. If we are to advance ourselves out of this mental and spiritual confusion, we must have the knowledge of what happened to our Ancient Egyptian ancestors in the past in order for us to know what has to be done in the future. If I had not written this book, chances are you would not have ever known the true historical origin of Islam. Islamic theology as taught throughout history and today will never reveal the true facts to you. Why? because the European and the European Arab religious and academic communities have erased the Coptic African Egyptian Monophysite origin of Islam either by ignorance or purposefully, thereby, creating a totally European and European Arab worldview of Islam.

Since we as an African people living in America have been spiritually disconnected from our Ancient Egyptian ancestors, we do not think and live our lives as subjects of our own ancestral historical experience. Therefore, we allow man to introduce to us one of his man-made spiritually dead unnatural religions.

I urge you to read and study this book very carefully. It will not be easy reading because of its unfamiliar terms, times, people and places. I have included a glossary and bibliography to assist the learning process. This book also will not be easy reading because of its untraditional and challenging perspective. Also, I am aware of the repetition in this book, but it is there to help you understand the message.

Belief is not necessarily knowledge. This statement will prove to be a worthwhile premise as you commence reading this book. Moreover, challenge your beliefs by doing personal research and looking for the facts that will provide knowledge and objectively to help determine whether your beliefs are TRUE.

Walter Williams
Founder of the Ancient Egyptian Museum
Founder - Society of New Scholars (SUNS)
Chicago, Illinois

CHAPTER I

THE COMING OF THE EUROPEANS IN AFRICA

One of the primary purposes of writing this book is to give the reader the step-by-step historical origin and realities of Monist Muhammedanism/Islam as opposed to the usual traditions, myths and fables. Tradition and other teachings simply have been passed on as truth and reality to succeeding generations throughout the centuries thus causing the initiated believer to invest his or her free Creator/Creatress-given spirituality into man-made religions such as Christianity, Islam, and Judaism. Today, as you look throughout the Islamic world you will find people of all nationalities who have changed their natural indigenous culture, names and customs trying to make these Islamic traditions, myths and fables into reality.

Before you read any further into this book, one dominant fact must be understood. This fact is that, to this day, there is no historical data or biography in existence to substantiate the life and times of a Traditional Prophet Muhammed of Islam ever living on earth in human form. Rather, researched evidence points to the use and distortion of the life of a real person who actually lived during a later time era to create the created creature, the Traditional Prophet of Islam. I will explain whom, when, and how as you read further in this book. Traditional religious Islam teaches myths, fables and stories that are connected to Islam for the believer to believe. The purpose of such teachings is to sustain the faith of the believer. As stated in the Shorter

Encyclopedia of Islam concerning this man created mythical creature named Muhammed, the Prophet (p.390), "In consequence of the unreliability of the sources at our disposal, the very first question a biographer has to ask, namely when was his hero born, cannot be answered with certainty."

The <u>hero</u> in the above quote is the traditional object of Islam; the created creature named Muhammed. But the main reason for not having historical data or a real life biography for a traditional Prophet Muhammed is because there never has been a man of traditional Islam that ever walked the earth in human form by the name of Muhammed, called the Prophet. Let us go a little deeper and find out how, when and where this created faceless icon came about. In order to do this, it became obvious that I would have to follow the Monophysites and the Dyophysitic Christian polemics or arguments throughout Byzantine history to the 13th Century when the human Muhammed emerged. As you read further in this book, I will introduce you to Ibn Al 'Arabi, the real Muhammed, the man whose biography and life were used to create the fictitious created character of Islamic tradition.

Before his introduction, I want to bring to your attention the world, as it was during the time of antiquity 10,000 B.C.E. to 332 B.C.E. During this time era, the Africans living throughout the continent of Africa practiced no religion. They did, however, practice what can be called an African traditional spiritual consciousness (ATSC), i.e., a spiritual way of life in tune with African spiritual thought and in tune with the cosmic rhythm of the universe. Included in this ancient African practice was an awareness of the omnipotent universal Creator/Creatress, respect for nature, paying homage and respect to their ancestors. Positive and negative forces were acknowledged in which all were done with certain rituals and libations that were offered in all three categories of ATSC. The Ancient Egyptians who had the world's first and oldest civilization were the first students of the universe and in their ancient African culture and civilization included the laws of Maat (truth, justice, peace, love and wisdom), the respect of the earth and its environments. Animals and nature also were included, and above all, respect, love, and homage paid to their royal ancestors. But this began to change with the coming of the uncivilized savage European invaders to the continent of Africa. The first known historical European to come was Alexander the Greek in 332 B.C.E.

Note that contrary to popular belief in today's African community, the Greeks prior to Alexander coming to Egypt did not study with the Ancient Egyptians in their sacred temples (institutions). The reasons: (1) Had the Greeks, studied with the Ancient Egyptians, the Greeks today would be bilingual, speaking Greek and the language of the Ancient Egyptians. (2) Greeks would have learned how The Great Pyramid was built. (3) They would have been taught the meaning of the Medu-Netcher (Hieroglyphic)symbols, <u>which never have been deciphered.</u> (read the revised ed. of The Historical Origin of Christianity appendix); and (4) The Greeks were a barbaric spiritually out of tune with the universe, illiterate people, and without an alphabet or any form of writing.

The Ancient Egyptians did not allow foreigners of any race into their sacred institutions. They were selective of their own African brothers and sisters, nor did they race mix during the time of antiquity. The Ancient Egyptians during the time of antiquity were the only people on earth who had a writing system is a fact that should not be over looked. They were the only literate people on earth. They created the first system of writing, Medu-Netcher, or Hieroglyphics, and the first alphabets, which are the Hieratic-Phonetic 1, and the Demotic-Phonetic 2.. (See alphabet chart on page 132) Read the revised edition of The Historical Origin of Christianity by this author, chapters 8 and 9 for more detailed information concerning the Greeks).

The Greeks and Romans who are one and the same race did begin studying with the Melchite Coptic Egyptians in Africa in Constantinople, Turkey after 537 A.C.E. in the Hagia Sophia. The Hagia Sophia is the world's first Christian church ever built and the first See or seat for Christianity. It was also the first European Institution and center of learning for Europeans. In this Institution, the teaching faculty was entirely Melchite Coptic African Egyptians. More will be said about the Hagia Sophia in Chapter Nine and about this period as you read further. After Alexander came to Africa, other European invaders began to enter the African continent.

They came from the Slavic areas of Europe such as Bulgaria, Albania, Yugoslavia, Hungary, Greece, Romania, areas of Southern Russia such as Azerbaijan, and Armenia. They used the Aegean, Bosporus, and Black Seas as their route to enter the geographical land areas in North Central and Northeast Africa, especially Turkey. The Mediterranean Sea was used to enter Egypt in Central Africa and other North African countries along the Mediterranean such as Libya, Tunisia, Algeria, Morocco, and Mauritania. Today these people are called Arabs. In Egypt, they were under the rule of the Greek Ptolomies. In Turkey, which included North Syria and the surrounding areas, they were under the rule of the Greek Seleucid rulers.

The Ptolomies and the Seleucid rulers were successors to Alexander the Greek after his death in 323 B.C.E. The Ptolomies, the Seleucid rulers, and other incoming Europeans invaded from Slavic Europe as aforementioned. All spoke an agglutinative Bulgarian/ Greek language form. Over the years, these Europeans began to migrate further south, west, and into the northeastern areas of the African continent into such places today known as Lebanon, Palestine, Jordan, Iraq, Iran (via Afghanistan), Saudi Arabia, and Yemen. Thus usurping the culture and customs of the indigenous Africans, and putting in its place their own uncivilized, savage European customs. Today, these same people have taken the traditional teachings of Islam and made them part of their customs and culture. The same also can be said of the African Islamic communities in Africa, America, and throughout the world today. I reiterate that before one can understand Monist Muhammedanism/Islam, one has to know ancient history and the historical origin of Christianity as well as Monophysite Christianity. But the most important fact to remember is that the traditional name Muhammed the Prophet is a name and title taken from Ibn Al' Arabi and given some of the attributes of Christ (borrowed from the Ancient Egyptian god, Osiris) after the death of Ibn Al' Arabi in 1240 A.C.E. Again, I recommend the reading of the revised edition of *The Historical Origin of Christianity* to further understand the origin of Christianity. I reiterate again that one has to realize that Monist Muhammedanism/Islam is a derivative of Monophysite Christianity before the historical origin of Monist Muhammedanism/Islam can be fully understood.

In Chapter II and Chapter V, I will introduce and explain Arianism, Monophysitism, Nestorianism, Monotheletism, Monothelitism, and Ibn Al' Arabi which collectively caused the creation of the name Muhammed and a new monist religion that was first called Muhammedanism now called Islam to come about. As you continue reading, keep in mind that Muhammed and Jesus are both created creatures. In order to understand Monist Muhammedanism/Islam or Christianity fully, one must know or study Ancient Egyptian and World History and understand how history progressed to the time, places, events, and dates for the creation of man created icons.

The difference is the icon of Christ has a face and the icon of Muhammed is faceless. In the case of Muhammed without a face, in Orthodox Islam it is against Islamic law to portray Muhammed with a face, which signifies a non-human creature, created by man. This gets to the heart of what was the ongoing polemic or argument between two factions, the Melchite Dyophysitic Coptic Egyptians and the Arianist/Monophysite Coptic Egyptians. The Melchite Copts created two dyophysitic natures (divine and human) for the creature Serapis/Christ (see *The Historical Origin of Christianity*, Chapter V, "The Council of Ephesus," by this author). At the same time the Monophysite Copts refused to accept the human nature that was given to Serapis/Christ at the Council of Ephesus in 431 A.B.C.E. However, they recognized only the divine Osiris-like spirit that was given to the Serapis icon by the Melchites in 320 B.C.E. This argument went on throughout the centuries for 921 years from the time Arius made his strong statement about the created creature Serapis in the year 319 A.B.C.E. Arius stated that Serapis who later became Christ was a created creature. This argument continued until the Monophysite faction became a racially mixed group of Africans and Europeans. As previously mentioned, today the European faction is called Arabs and they are living throughout Northeast Africa (Turkey, Syria, Jordan, Iran (via Afghanistan) Iraq, Saudi Arabia, Yemen, Lebanon, Palestine, etc.), Central Africa (Egypt) and all the countries of North Africa that border the Mediterranean sea. This Monophysitic African and

European faction in the 13th century starting with the disciples and followers of Ibn Al' Arabi alias Muhammed began to use his biography and life to create and fashion a new monist religion called Muhammedanism. Centuries later the religion would be called Islam. The change was consummated when the religion was officially named Islam during and after the formulation and writing of the world's first Koran based on the first five books (by Moses) and Psalms of the Old Testament and the Four Gospels of the New Testament. This effort began in 1870 in Syria and finished 49 years later and accepted by the Muhammedan world in 1919 at Cairo, Egypt. It was at this point that they ceased calling the religion Muhammedanism.

Armed with new literature, "The Koran", written and formulated by Jewish scholars from the Jewish Organization, The Alliance Israelite Universal of Paris, France together with Christian scholars, a new religion called "Islam" was created. The Koran and Islam were approved by Arab scholars who began to create more tradition for their newly formed Islamic religion along with more traditional manufactured stories attached to the created Muhammed. One of the first things the Arab scholars did was to give a special praise to the name Muhammed whenever this name was spoken, thus invoking what is known as Haqiqa Al-Muhammediyya (Haqiqa means to sing the praises of Muhammed). A tradition was established. Even more tradition connected to the name Muhammed was created by Jewish scholars, which is known as Israiliyat or Israelite tales. For example, according to tradition, Muhammed, the Prophet, was illiterate, and therefore, not able to read. Hence, according to tradition, the Angel Gabriel taught him the entire Koran and, subsequently, Muhammed dictated the Koran to a scribe from memory. Let us take a look and find out who this Angel Gabriel is supposed to be. If you take the time and investigate, you will discover that the Angels Gabriel is a little bird and further inquiry reveals that another angel, Israfil, taught Gabriel. Israfil is described as a six tongue hairy monster. More will be said about the Archangels Gabriel and Israfil as you read further in this book. This is what Islamic tradition is teaching its adherents to believe. In the following chapter, I will continue to reveal to the reader how the Monophysitic and Dyophysitic feud eventually led to Ibn Al' Arabi Alias Muhammed whose biography and life were used to create Muhammed, the Prophet of Islam.

CHAPTER II

LAYING THE FOUNDATION FOR
THE CREATION OF THE NAME MUHAMMED

In order to understand the man-made religion called Islam, previously known as Muhammedanism, it is essential to understand that Islam, is nothing more than a derivative of earliest Christianity or Monophysite Christianity. Through various iterations and events, the development of Monist Muhammedanism/Islam unfolded over the centuries through various movements such as Arianism, Monophysitism, Nestorianism, Christianity, Monotheletism, Monothelitism, and more. Briefly, I will explain the central thought of each movement.

First: Arianism = A strong statement by the Coptic Egyptian Arius (280-336) in 319 A.B.C.E. Arius spoke out against Serapis and Sylvester I who accepted the donation of Constantine from the Emperor Constantine I. Arius stated that the created creature, Serapis, who today is called Jesus The Christ was a created creature "alien and dissimilar in all things from the father (Osiris) a perfect creature above all other created creatures, but a creature nevertheless." This started what is known today in history as Arianism, the world's first religious controversy that laid the foundation for Monophysitism, Nestorianism, and the first Ecumenical Council ever held "The Council of Nicaea I" in 325 A.B.C.E. Note, Osiris is the father in the Ancient Egyptian Divine Triad (Osiris,

Isis, and Horus the Sun).

Second: Monophysitism - The true meaning of Monophysitism comes from the father of Monophysitism, the Coptic Egyptian Eutyches (378-454). He taught that Serapis who today is Jesus The Christ had only one Osiris-like spirit, but <u>no human nature</u>.

Third: Nestorianism – Originated with the Coptic Egyptian, Nestorius (373-451), who could not accept the title of Theotokas (the Mother of God) for the created creature the Virgin Mary. Note <u>God</u> in the title of Theotokas is referring to Serapis who today is known as Jesus the Christ.

Fourth: Monotheletism (one will) was first proposed in the year 622 A.C.E. and was immediately adopted by the Emperor Heraclius I, for political reasons, as a compromise between Monophysitism and Chalcedonian orthodoxy (Christianity). It was designed to settle the argument over the supposed human nature of Christ by using the words <u>one will</u> as opposed to no human nature.

Fifth: Monothelitism ("one energy") is also called Monoenergism. It is a formula that was first produced by the African Monophysite Bishop Sergius I, Patriarch of Constantinople (C.633), who had the strong support of the Coptic Egyptian Monophysite Cyrus Patriarch of Egypt. Sergius introduced a formula that stated that in Christ there was only one energy proceeding from a unique will.

I will now walk you through the process of 921 years of the Byzantine era and introduce you to the time, people, places and events that caused the creation of the coming of Ibn Al 'Arabi alias <u>Muhammed</u> in the thirteenth century. Let us pick up the ongoing feud between the African Monophysites and the African Chalcedonian Orthodox Christians and focus in on the time of the Byzantine era and the Roman Byzantine ruler <u>Zeno</u> (474-491). During his reign, Zeno tried to reconcile the Monophysites to the decrees of the Council of Chalcedon (451) through the <u>Henoticon</u>. The Coptic Egyptian Monophysite Acacius, the patriarch of Constantinople, composed this epistolary decree that was issued by Zeno in 482. This decree of union that Zeno promulgated was intended to conclude the Christological disputes between the Monophysites and the Chalcedonian Orthodox Christians.

The Henoticon decree cited the authority of the first four Ecumenical Councils, Nicaea I (325), Constantinople I (381), and Ephesus (431) that condemned Nestorius and Eutyches, and the Council of Chalcedon that affirmed the consubstantiality of Christ with God (Osiris) and with man. Interestingly, the decree skillfully avoided the Chalcedonian use of the terms "nature and person." Composed by Acacius with the support of the Coptic Egyptian Bishop Peter Mongus and promulgated by Zeno, this decree caused such a strong resistance and schism among the two opposing factions that today in history it is known as the "Acacian Schism" (484-519). Keep in mind that the feud was whether the Christian object, Christ, had a human nature. The Monophysites said that Christ had no human nature. Conversely, the Chalcedonian Orthodox Christians said that Christ had two natures, a divine-Osiris like spirit and a human nature. As a side note, keep in mind that the two feuding communities were Coptic Egyptian Africans. Other non-indigenous races living within the African Continent were not involved in this philosophical wrangling at this time in history. This wrangling should lead one to the question; if this Christ was a real life human being (person), then why was there an ongoing argument over the human nature of this Christian object? Remember that these polemics between the Monophysites and the Dyophysites were laying the foundation for the eventual coming of the monist Ibn Al' Arabi in the 13th century. And, the use of his alias, <u>Muhammed</u>, that was given to him by his disciples and followers that would later be applied to the man-made religions, Muhammedanism and <u>Islam</u>. Let us move a little further in time and history and come into the time of the Byzantine Roman ruler, <u>Anastasius I</u> (Anu sta_'shus) (491-518).

Anastasius, the successor of Zeno, tried to pamper the Monophysites, which caused more religious unrest among the two Coptic Egyptian factions throughout the Byzantine Roman Empire. He also caused unrest among the large European community living in and around Constantinople, Turkey, the seat of the Byzantine Roman government. Anastasius stopped the gladiator competition in the Hippodrome (stadium) in the year before his death in 517 A.C.E. This action caused civil and political unrest among the two sports minded factions of Europeans living in the geographical area of Northeast Africa, Constantinople, Turkey.

These two sports oriented demes or factions were called the Venetis and the Prasinis, i.e., the Greens and Blues. Each faction had its own color emblem identity just like the ball clubs of today. These factions or demes of the Hippodrome occupied the benches at the end of the arena on each side adjacent to the kathisma (the name given to the seat occupied by the emperor when viewing the different sporting events held in the Hippodrome).

The gladiator competition was one of the most popular of all events presented in the Hippodrome. By abolishing this savage event, Anastasius became very unpopular among the Europeans living in Constantinople and the surrounding areas. Imagine the President of the United States of America abolishing football. This would cause total chaos in America. The abolition of the gladiator competition set the stage for two important historical events, the Nikka riots in the year 532 under the rule of Justinian I and his wife Theodora and the evangelizing of the Europeans by the quasi-Monophysite Coptic African Christians. Both events will be explained in more detail as we progress.

We now move to the time of the Byzantine Roman Emperor, Justin I (518-527), successor of Anastasius I.

He was an anti-Monophysite who also kept the abolishment of the gladiator competition enforced until his death in 527. Succeeding Justin I to the throne was his nephew, Justinian I (527-565), along with his wife Theodora. In addition to being faced with the decisions of their predecessors, a number of important events would happen in history during the reign of Justinian I and Theodora. For example, in the year 532, the same year that Justinian and Theodora commissioned African Egyptian architects to build the world's First Christian Church and the world's first European University, the Hagia Sophia, the Nikka riots occurred in Constantinople, Turkey. Keep in mind that these Europeans were still angry over the Emperor Anastasius I abolishing the gladiator competition 15 years earlier.

In January 532, a disturbance broke out between the two factions, the Greens and the Blues. The ringleader of each party was punished. In response, the two rival factions united in armed revolt against the Byzantine government. Open violence erupted as the government cracked down on both factions. The city was filled with fire, bloodshed, murder, and looting. Thousands of people were slain in the rioting. The crowd cried out "Nikka" (Greek for "conquer"). This is recorded in history as the "Nikka riots." The city of Constantinople was out of control and Justinian's life and power stood in jeopardy. He decided to abdicate and prepared to abandon his capital by ship. But at the last moment, Empress Theodora, in a bold speech, turned the tide of her husband's fears. Her firm stand aroused new determination in Justinian. He decided to stand his ground. Justinian dispatched Belisarius, his army general, to the Hippodrome stadium with 3,000 soldiers whom slaughtered 30,000 people. The day after the riots, the rioters were suppressed. Justinian's throne was saved. It was at this point that Justinian began to take full control of his African Byzantine Eastern Roman government. He viewed political and ecclesiastical policies as being inextricably linked. A number of years later after he finished building the Hagia Sophia (532-537), Justinian prepared himself to take back the Donation of Constantine, which he did later at the Council of Constantinople II in 553. Justinian knew that this maneuver would give him the Ecclesiastical and political power that he needed to become the head papa or pope of this Church and University. He was advised by his legal counselor, the Coptic Egyptian, Theodore Ascidas, as to how to take back "the Donation of Constantine." In 543 A.C.E., Ascidas advised Justinian to condemn "The Three Chapters" which were the anti-Monophysitic writings of Theodore of Mopsuestia, Theodoret of Cyr and Ibas of Edessa. All three writings were against the position of the quasi-Christian Monophysite Nestorius who could not accept the title of "Theotokos" given to the created creature, The Virgin Mary at the Council of Ephesus. These writings were used in the dogmatic decrees at the Councils of Ephesus (431) and Chalcedon (451). The plot included the attempt to get Vigilius, the African

Patriarch, who had complete ecclesiastical authority via the Donation of Constantine to condemn "The Three Chapters" and take Holy Communion with the Monophysites. Justinian and Ascidas knew that Vigilius would refuse. His refusal would give Justinian an excuse to take back the Donation of Constantine by force, thus giving himself full ecclesiastical and political authority over the Church of Hagia Sophia. This also would allow him to practice Ceasaropapism over his Byzantine eastern African Empire. Justinian believed that his strategy would culminate in the destruction and elimination of the feud between the Monophysites and the Christian Dyophysitic Coptic Egyptians once and for all. As you read further, you will see that history proved Justinian wrong.

With complete political authority and now full ecclesiastical power after the disposal of Vigilius in 555, Justinian had attained the two major aspects of his envisioned Christian Empire. However, two things hampered his vision, the on-going feud between the Coptic Egyptian Monophysites and the Dyophysitic Melchite Copts and the unrest among the Europeans living in Constantinople. Given these issues, Justinian and Theodora had their work cut out for them. After the riot Theodora took the suggestion and request of the wealthy European Prince Harith Ibn Gabala in 543 to send someone to evangelize among the Europeans and other non-Africans living in Constantinople and other surrounding areas in Northeast Africa. This was done after Justinian and his army successfully put down the

Nikka riots in 532. Boasted by their victory, Justinian and the Empress Theodora tried unsuccessfully to get the rioters to accept Christianity.

In the meantime Theodora called on Jacob Baradaeus, A.K.A. James Baradai, one of her controlled Coptic quasi-Monophysites of whom she favored. In 543, Theodora, after honoring the request of Harith Ibn Gabala, ordered Bishop Jacob Baradaeus to evangelize among and convert the Europeans who, today, are called Arabs to Monophysite Christianity. Theodora most likely was thinking that a half Christian was better than none at all. For this purpose, Baradaeus, a compromising Monophysite consecrated a large number of compromising Syrian African Monophysites as bishops, priests and other clergy, including women who were called virgins, to help in this missionary work among the Europeans. Keep in mind the African Monophysite community and the African Orthodox Christian community practiced celibacy. Later this practice of celibacy was transferred to Europe via the Roman Catholic Church following the fall of Constantinople and the Church of Hagia Sophia in 1453.

Continuing with Justinian and Theodora, that same year, 543, Justinian and Theodora, six years before her death in 549, began to build the world's <u>first Coptic Christian Church,</u> which was a Monophysite Church. Today this is the Jacobite Church in Syria, named after Jacob Baradaeus some years after it was built. It was used as the main headquarters for the missionary work done by Jacob Baradaeus among the Europeans, today referred to as Muslim Arabs. This helped Baradaeus to establish a new hierarchy among the Coptic Egyptian Monophysites, but not all African Monophysites were in favor of this move thereby causing more unrest among the Monophysite community. This was the first time in world history that Europeans became involved in a religious dispute after being introduced to Monophysite Christianity, which later evolved and became the foundation for Monist Muhammedanism/Islam.

Monophysitism began to spread in later years to other European communities in Northeast Africa, North Africa along the Mediterranean, parts of Central Africa or Egypt, and in the Balkan areas of Europe. These areas represented the Byzantine Christian Empire and later the Ottoman Empire that embraced Monist Muhammadenism. In later years, these Europeans used their monophysitic teachings to attack the Roman Byzantine government. In doing so, they threatened the destruction of the Hagia Sophia in Constantinople. This violent campaign lasted until the Ottoman Turks totally destroyed the Byzantine Empire in 1453. More will be said about the European Monophysites as we progress.

Let's continue the historical route that helped to create the traditional name Muhammed and the traditional doctrine for Islam. This brings us to the time of the Byzantine Roman Emperor Justin II (565-578), the nephew and successor of Justinian I. He too had no tolerance for the Monophysites. In 572, he began a severe persecution of the Monophysites that lasted until he lost his reasoning ability (mind) in 574. His adopted son, Tiberius, exercised the rule of the government, keeping the pressure on the Monophysites until the death of Justin in 578. Tiberius then succeeded to the throne and continued the pressure on the Monophysites until his death in 582.

Note: The Monophysites are now racially mixed with Coptic Egyptians and Europeans. The European Monophysite community, which was started by the evangelizing of the African Copt, Jacob Baradaeus, was physically violent as opposed to the nonviolent philosophical wrangling of the Coptic African Monophysites.

After the death of Tiberius, this brought Mauricius or Maurice (582-602) to the throne as Emperor. His reign of 20 years was occupied with Monophysitic dealings and other government turmoil that lasted until Phacas usurped him. Proclaimed as emperor in 602 Phacas reigned for eight years until Heraclius I (610-641) became the new Byzantine Emperor. He sought to reconcile the African Syrians and the Coptic Egyptian Monophysites with the Orthodox Christian Church (the Hagia Sophia) by adopting the doctrines of Monotheletism (one will) and Monothelitism (one energy). These doctrines declared that Christ operated with but one will or one energy although having two natures. This theology, however, opposed the intent of the Council of Chalcedon (451).

Monotheletism was first proposed in 622 and was immediately adopted by the Emperor Heraclius I. For political reasons, his thinking possibly was that this formula could be used as a compromise between the Monophysites and Orthodoxy. However, both sides did not agree. Honorius I, Patriarch of the Hagia Sophia, by Ecclesiastical authority of the Emperor Heraclius I supported one will, but forbade further discussion of the question. Soon afterwards, Heraclius, using a revised Monothelite thesis of the Coptic Monophysite, Sergius I, Patriarch of Constantinople, who, with the strong support of Cyrus, Patriarch of Egypt, formulated a compromising thesis (C.633) that took the position that Christ had one operation or will, but with one energy. As a result, in 638 Heraclius published the Ectheis, which defined Monothelitism as the official imperial form of Christianity. While Heraclius I was appeasing the African Monophysites, the Slavic European Monophysites were beginning to attack his Empire.

Let me present a short historical overview concerning the Slavic European Monophysite communities today called Muslims and Arabs. These Slavic communities were in Constantinople and throughout Northeast Africa. They spoke the dominant language Greek along with other Slavic dialects. For the first time after being introduced to the Monophysite teachings by Jacob Baradaes in 543, they began violent attacks on the Byzantine government thus causing the Byzantine Emperor Heraclius to withdraw from Syria in 636. In the following year, 637, the capital Ctesiphon-Seleucia in the Arabian/Iraq region fell and its Byzantine overseers fled for their lives. In 641, the Byzantine garrisons in Egypt fell to a Slavic

European Monophysite army. The importance of pointing this out is because in today's history books, we are told that Egypt during this time in history (641) was invaded by the Arabs and it was in Egypt where the Arabs first introduced the religion known today as Islam. As you read further, you will see this to be untrue.

The previous point is untrue because Egypt along with Ethiopia, Syria, and all other areas outside of Constantinople were Monophysitic during this time in history (641). Let it be noted that Christianity was practiced mainly by the Melchite community via the Church of Hagia Sophia in Constantinople. Moreover, Islam is a religion based upon a book called the Koran and was created many years later. Without the Koran there would not be any Islam as a religion.

Heraclius' successors, Constantine III and Constans II (642-668), continued to enforce Monothelitism with the Ectheis. This went against the powerless Patriarchs of the Hagia Sophia. All Patriarchs of the Hagia Sophia were Africans and powerless because complete ecclesiastical authority was by then in the hands of the Byzantine emperors due to the Donation of Constantine (313-314). Before Heraclius died, he worked out an agreement with the patriarchs of the African Syrian Jacobite Church concerning the Monothelet Doctrine (one will) by agreeing on the term Monoenergism (Monothelite) (one energy) in Christ. With this new formula, "will" was substituted for "energy." Constans II after disposing of Constantine III withdrew the Ectheis and Monoenergism and promulgated instead the Typus or Typos, a decree flatly forbidding the mention of one will or two wills or one energy or two energies in the second person of Christ.

The Typus was intended to make peace among the African Monophysites and the African Orthodox Christians, but instead brought on more crises to the controversy. In the meantime the aggression of the European Arabs within the Empire continued. From 647 to 667 Slavic Europeans from the Balkans and other areas of Europe began organizing war parties that were raiding Byzantine North Africa. They established a permanent base in Tunisia.

Keep in mind that the history that I am writing about in this book laid the foundation for the biography and life of Ibn Al 'Arabi, alias Muhammed, to be used to create the new religion called Muhammedanism. This religion later evolved into Islam for the African and European Monophysite community in Africa in the 20th century. Let me also reiterate. Regarding the created creature Christ, the question must be raised again that if there was a man who walked the earth in human form by the name of Jesus the Christ, then why was there such a strong polemic or argument about the human nature of one such icon?

Let's move to our next Byzantine Emperor Constantine IV (668-685), son of Constantine III. In his efforts to deal with the Monophysites and other ecclesiastical problems, he called the Council of Constantinople III to order which started in November 680 and lasted until September 681. This Council is referred to as the first Trullan Council. It

was convoked to do the following: (A) Condemn the Monophysites, Monotheletism and Monothelitism;
(B) Condemn the powerless Patriarch of the Hagia Sophia Honorius I for tolerating the Monothelite formula of the Patriarchs Sergius I and Cyrus;
(C) Restore peace with the Christian religious community in Rome (West) and the Hagia Sophia (East); and
(D) Formulate a decree of faith that proclaimed the doctrine of the two wills and the two natural energies in Christ, undivided, inseparable, and without confusion.
The Emperor signed this doctrine as well as the 178 council members making this decree official. But during his reign as Emperor he was under constant attack by the Europeans in Bulgaria that lasted until he conceded the territory to them located south of the Danube where they established their kingdom in 679. This gave Constantine's rule as Emperor six years of peace until he died in 683. I will continue the discussion of the European Byzantine Emperors in Chapter III.

CHAPTER III

THE COUNCIL OF NICAEA II
IMAGE MAKING VERSUS ICONOCLASM
THE ICONOCLAST CONTROVERSY

We now come to the Byzantine rule of Justinian II (685-711), son and successor of Constantine IV. Justinian unsuccessfully warred against the European Monophysites within the Empire. This era of Byzantine rule by Justinian was marred by repeated attacks against Constantinople, the Byzantine capital in Turkey. During the last year of the rule of Justinian, the Saracen Monophysite Arabs from North Africa expanded their attacks to include the invasion of Spain in 711. Modern history books are calling this group of European Saracen Monophysites "Moors" and go on to say that they took "Islam" to Spain and forced this supposed religion on the people of Spain. History also is saying that they are called Moors because they entered Spain from Mauritania and Morocco in North Africa. I repudiate this misinformation that the Saracen Arabs brought Islam to Spain in 711 which unfortunately continues to be disseminated today to the world populous.

I will present the facts and make the case that in 711 there was no religion called Islam. Islam is a religion based upon a book called the Koran which was first formulated in Syria in 1870 and accepted by the Arab Muhammedan world in Cairo, Egypt in 1919. Perhaps, a more accurate scenario is that the Monophysite Arabs tried to force Monophysitism on the people of Spain in 711.

Note: Spain was a non-religious pagan country during this time.

Let's get back to Justinian. In the last year of the rule of Justinian, a series of usurpers occupied the throne from 711 to 717 until Leo III established a new dynasty (717-741). Leo shattered the Arab Monophysite attacks on Constantinople in 717, saving the Empire and the Hagia Sophia. By keeping the non-Christian European Monophysites from penetrating Constantinople and seizing the Hagia Sophia, the world's first Christian Church and learning center for Europeans, Leo kept the religion of Christianity from being totally destroyed, and hence saved the empire as a whole. Leo then went on to form a truce with the Arab Monophysite leader Umar Ibn'Abd Al'-Aziz in the same year 717.

Prior to Leo becoming the new Byzantine Emperor, Byzantium had many usurpers as aforementioned that included Philippicus (711 to 713). During his reign Philippicus had his portrait painted and put on display throughout the eastern areas of the empire to show himself as the new emperor. This gave the Patriarch of the Hagia Sophia Constantine I (708-715), the devious idea of having an icon (image) of Christ put on display for the purpose of combating the Monophysite doctrine that taught that Christ had but one Osiris like assimilated spirit but no human nature. Constantine I introduced this devious idea to the incoming Dyophysitic Patriarch Gregory III (715-731) who tried to engage the new

Monophysite Patriarch of Constantinople, Germanus I (715-730), to this idea. Germanus refused to go along with this thought. At this point, Gregory III began to commission artists to paint icons of Christ for the purpose of display. The iconic display created a symbolic pictorial language in visible form to insinuate in pictorial form that Christ was a human being having a human nature, i.e., displaying Christ as God-man. These painted icons of Christ were frontal, lacking in shadows and laconic which means to express much in a few words. This takes me to the old adage that a picture is worth a thousand words.

The issuing of painted icons of Christ by the Patriarch Gregory III went against the ecclesiastical and political authority of Emperor Leo III who like all Byzantine emperors before him had complete ecclesiastical and political authority over the Hagia Sophia and its Patriarchs. This authority harked back to the "Donation of Constantine" that was given to the Melchite African, Sylvester I by the Emperor Constantine I in 313-314 A.B.C.E. and later taken back by Justinian in 553. (See the Historical Origin of Christianity) Leo III and his advisors opposed the views of Gregory III on the veneration of images. To counter at that point, Leo in 724 asked two African Monophysite clergymen, Constantine the Black and Thomas, who both lived in Constantinople, to formulate a decree to combat this illegal iconic display.

The decree that was formulated by the two African clergymen is known today in history as "iconoclasm"or "image breaking." The Emperor at once adopted this formula. Without his support it would have had no future. In 725-726 the Emperor Leo III enforced an order that mandated the abolition of images. In 726 he ordered the figure of Christ surmounting the Chalke palace gate to be removed.

Finally, by pressing Gregory in a solemn audience to sign a decree against images, he, in effect, forced the patriarch to resign on January 7, 730. Leo then enforced the iconoclasm decree to keep the violent European Saracen Monophysites from disrupting his Byzantine East African Roman government. This was all done to honor the truce by Leo and Umar Ibn'Abd Al'-Aziz in 717. To further the readers understanding of Iconoclasm, let's take a closer look.

The term iconoclasm refers to extreme opposition to the representation of the human figure and veneration of the Christ image (icon), the two being held inseparable. Iconoclasm in its Christian context is especially associated with a period in the history of the Byzantine African Roman Empire that can be divided into three discernable phases. The first division began with its emergence under emperors Leo III (717-741) and Constantine V (741-775), and the iconoclastic "Council of Hiereia" in 754, the second division was the Ecumenical Council of Nicaea II (787), and, third, its restoration and final extinction in 815-842. As you read further I will explain the above aforementioned events.

Note: I reemphasize, what you have read thus far in this book is some of the 921 years of history that it took to get to the time of Ibn Al 'Arabi. He is the real person whose biography and life were used to create the created creature, the Prophet Muhammed, for traditional Islam.

This brings us to the Byzantine rule of Constantine V (741-775), the son of Leo III. He also sought to have images condemned via his power of ecclesiastical authority through the Donation of Constantine in which he imposed iconoclasm as a duty of conscience as well as an obligation for all citizens to abide. In 752 he elaborated on an original theology against images, that he developed into treatises and which he, like his father, defended in public audiences. Two years later, he had it ratified in a General Council of the Byzantine Episcopate (338 council members attending) held in the suburban palace of Hiereia (754). The definition of iconoclasm prepared by this Council which was proclaimed "ecumenical" has been preserved in the acta of the eigth council called (Nicaea II 787). They then went on to denounce all pictorial representation of Christ as idols. Initially, the authorities showed a certain moderation in effecting the anti-image decisions of the Emperor at the Council of Hiereia. Nevertheless, violent repression of the opposition did not occur until a dozen years later.

In 761, the monk, Andrew of Crete, was executed and in 765 persecution again broke out in full force. The recluse, Stephen the Younger, promoted a movement hostile to the Council of Hiereia, some few miles outside of Constantinople. Among his followers was many of the elite of Constantinople's society. The Patriarch of the Hagia Sophia Constantine II himself (754-766) was lukewarm in applying the imperial edicts, which caused the Emperor to suspect a cabal or even a plot. On November 20, 765, Stephen the Monk was killed on the orders of the Emperor. Shortly thereafter the Emperor imposed a loyalty oath to promote his imperial policy. The following summer of 766 he humiliated all monks and all other anti-iconoclasm clergy by putting on a grotesque parade in the Hippodrome. He even attacked members of his own entourage. He followed this up by secularizing any monastery where he encountered resistance. Simultaneously he placed loyal generals in command of key military areas in Asia Minor (Turkey). Monks were dispersed from Ephesus and other key areas throughout Asia Minor giving them a choice between mutilation and exile after which he confiscated all monastic property. Iconoclasm had thus evolved by force of circumstances into a war of Monasticism, although they were two distinct movements.

We now come to the time of the second major division of iconoclasm and the reign of Byzantine Emperor Leo IV (775-780), son and successor of Constantine V. He resumed the iconoclastic policy of his father and grandfather Leo III. On Leo's mysterious death, his wife, Irene, became regent and co-ruler with their young ten-year-old son, Constantine VI, 780-797. She strongly supported the veneration of images and began to move with caution to reverse the iconoclastic policies of her late husband, Leo IV, by removing his entire administration one by one. In 787, Irene convened the eighth Ecumenical Council, the Council of Nicaeae II, August to October 787. Irene was determined to restore the veneration of icons throughout the empire, a practice forbidden in Byzantium for more than 61 years. The entire state government was in the hands of men committed to iconoclasm. A plot to get rid of Irene was vigorously repressed, enabling her to remove administrators and other high government personages who were hostile to iconduly. She then contacted the Patriarch of the Hagia Sophia, Adrian I, informing him of the intention of the Byzantine government to convoke a general council and requested him to send representatives from the west (Rome). She then removed the main obstacle to such a council. This was the Monophysite Patriarch of Constantinople, Paul IV, whom was replaced as patriarch by the empress's own secretary Tarasius. This infuriated the Monophysites. Remember, iconoclasm was enforced by the Byzantine government during this time in history to keep peace with the savage Saracen Monophysite Arabs who were a constant threat to the peace in that region of the world in Africa. The order convoking the council was promulgated throughout the Northeast African Byzantine Empire at the beginning of 786. Two members of the Roman clergy were sent to represent the west (Rome). The Byzantine Eastern Episcopate sent 350 of its members.

On August 1, 786, the council opened in

Constantinople in the Hagia Sophia, but hostile elements of the imperial guard broke into the Church, forcing the Council's temporary dissolution. This forced Irene, along with her Prime Minister Stravrakios, to disband all regiments that had mutinied. This disturbance caused the Empress to transfer the Council to Nicaea in Bithynia, where it opened on September 24 in 787. The sessions, eight in all, lasted three weeks, and all except the last were held at Irene's Imperial Magnaura Palace in Constantinople. The newly appointed Patriarch Tarasius of Constantinople presided, but Patriarch Adrian I of the Hagia Sophia signed all documents first and was always listed first. The Council had to decide immediately about the iconoclastic Bishops, of whom many were present. Could the council recognize their right to be seated? It took the first three sessions to dispose of this burning question for the monks who were numerous and who actively - opposed the council's decision to recognize the iconoclastic Bishops once they had adjured their iconoclastic thoughts before the assembly. The next two sessions (October 1 and 4) established the position of legitimacy for the veneration of icons. The sixth session (October 5 and 6) dealt with Tarasius's demand that the great synod held at Hiereia in 754 be condemned. The seventh session held October 13 climaxed the debate.

The terms were fixed by the dogmatic decree that proclaimed belief in the efficacy of the intercession, i.e., an interceding, mediation, pleading or prayer. On behalf of another which was to be done by the intercession of saints and to the adoration of the icon of Christ as God alone. Twenty-two disciplinary canons were appended to this dogmatic definition. The Empress, with ulterior political motives, wished to associate the people of the capital city, Constantinople, with the decisions of the council, and therefore decided to close the council at Nicaea by issuing a decree designed by Tarasius that deified the image of Christ.

For an eighth session, Irene decided to move the council to her Magnaura palace in Constantinople on October 23 where she addressed the assembly of bishops and clergy and thus had the Decree of Faith proclaimed. Irene and the attending Bishops signed the Decree. The acts of the Council then became the law of the Byzantine Empire. The council thus marked the end of the first period of iconoclasm. Irene had completed her personal goal of venerating the icon of Christ, which ended her campaign against iconoclasm. Irene was later deposed by her finance minister, Nicephorus I, and died in exile in 802. Nicephorus I (802-811) became the new emperor and kept the battle against iconoclasm enforced. Nicephorus was killed in battle while fighting against the Bulgarian Greeks and was succeeded by his son-in-law, Michael I.

Michael I (811-813) became the new Byzantine emperor. He supported Christian Orthodoxy against iconoclasm. Two years after becoming emperor, he was defeated by the Bulgarians, deposed and went into exile. Leo V was then proclaimed emperor (813-820). During his reign, he made peace with the Bulgarian Greeks who supported iconoclasm and who had a helping hand in deposing the two Byzantine Emperors before him, Nicephorus I and Michael I. Leo was concerned that after the death of the Bulgarian king Krum (April 14, 814), the siege of Constantinople would be imminent. To safe guard against this, Leo arranged a 30-year peace treaty with the New Greek Bulgarian King Khan Omortag (815-816). This treaty ended the second period of iconoclasm and initiated the third period of iconoclasm.

Leo set up a commission of six to justify the iconoclastic theology in a document that repudiated the making, the existence and veneration of images. He exiled the Patriarch of the Hagia Sophia, Nicephorus, from Constantinople for his opposition to iconoclasm. In his place, Leo installed Theodotus as the new patriarch and convoked a synod in the Hagia Sophia (April 815) to confirm the decisions of Constantine V's council of 754, "Council of Hiereia," and condemn the justification of the use of images defined by the council of "Nicaea II" (787). He persecuted all bishops and clergy for their opposition to his iconoclastic policy. This brought on Michael II (820-829) as the next Byzantine Emperor after his supporters had assassinated Leo in the palace chapel in Constantinople.

Michael had an indifferent attitude towards religious controversy. He tolerated both Orthodoxy and iconoclasm. Late in his reign, however, he actively supported iconoclasm. During this time, he kept the

Monophysites pampered. His son, Theophilus (829-842), who continued iconoclasm enforcement throughout the empire, succeeded Michael. His iconoclastic decrees were directed mainly against the opposing monks whom he made examples, many by burning iconoclastic verses on their foreheads. Hence, they were called the "inscribed." After the death of Theophilus, his son Michael III (842-867), succeeded the throne when still a child under the regency of his mother, the Empress Theodora II. She put an end to the last remnants of iconoclasm. She restored the peace of the Church (the Hagia Sophia) with the west (Rome, Germany and France), and took strong measures against the spread of the Bogomilian Heresy.

The Bogomils were a Monphysite Docetist group living in Bulgaria under Byzantine Rule. They professed that Christ did not have a human body, but only the appearance of one. Her actions brought on renewed war with the Saracen Arabs. This called for efficient military leadership that Theodora and her Ministers were unable to provide. In 856, Michael, aided by his maternal uncle Bardas, overthrew his mother, Theodora's Regency, forcing her into a convent. At this point, Bardas became the real ruler of the Empire. In 858, the Patriarch Ignatius of Constantinople was compelled to resign. Subsequently, the Monophysite Greek speaking Layman, Photius of Constantinople, replaced him. This was done to appease the Monophysite Saracen Arabs and the Balkan Slavs who were upset over the actions of Empress Theodora II.

In 861 the Legates of the Patriarch of the Hagia Sophia, Nicholas I, approved the election of Photius who was rushed within a week through the orders necessary to fill his position. This procedure which was non-canonical, but without precedent caused the Patriarch Nicholas I to refuse recognition of Photius. This caused Photius to retaliate by calling a Synod in 861. Several significant decisions were made at this Synod. The first, Photius challenged the interference of Nicholas I concerning the ecclesiastical authority of the Emperor Bardas for appointing him Patriarch of Constantinople. Secondly, Photius made public his refusal to practice celibacy. Lastly, he made public his refusal to accept the inclusion of the Filioque in the Creed. The Filioque means the created son, Serapis/Christ being inserted into the Homoousios Creed or Nicene Creed as being the same as with the Father (Osiris), i.e., "God the father, God the Son, the Same." This took place at the Council of Nicaea I in 325 A.B.C.E. when the Melchite Copts removed Horus from the Ancient Egyptian Divine Triad and inserted Serapis/Christ in his place. This 861 Synod caused the Photius-Filioque controversy to come into historical existence. While the controversy raged, in the meantime, Byzantine power and authority continued to be threatened by the Arabs. The Balkan Slavs and now the Russians began to attack the Empire from across the Black Sea. This made the position of the Empire extremely precarious. Michael III realizing that his Uncle

Bardas like his mother lacked the ability for government and military leadership had him murdered in his presence by Basil in 866. Basil then became co-Emperor.

In 867 Basil murdered Michael and thus became Basil I, founder of the Macedonian (Armenian Dynasty – 867-886). As soon as he was Master of the Byzantine Empire, his rule of authority was endangered by the on-going religious dissentions. He started a resolution to regulate the quarrel that was dividing the Byzantine Church (Hagia Sophia) in which he tried to normalize the relation of this church with the Patriarch of Constantinople. Basil deposed Photius for having dared to censure him and reinstated Ignatius as Patriarch of Constantinople.

Ignatius asked Basil for permission to convoke what is known in History as the Council of Constantinople IV (869-870). The Council opened in the Hagia Sophia October 05, 869. Photius was required to appear twice on October 20 and 29. On his second appearance (The 7th Session), Photius was anathematized together with his supporters. A week later, at the 8th session, all of the writings relating to the Synod called for by Photius in the summer of 861 were solemnly burned. On February 28, 870, twenty- seven disciplinary canons were issued and signed by the Emperor, the attending legates of the three Eastern Patriarchs, and by Ignatius. This proclaimed an imperial edict that promulgated (870) the decisions of the Council as laws of the Byzantine Empire. The Council also focused on how to deal with the Monophysite community that was still fighting and arguing over the veneration of the image of the Christ icon. The image was still under attack by the Monophysite community in and around the Balkans, Turkey, Syria, and other areas of North and Northeast Africa, including Egypt and Ethiopia. The continuous quarrels by the African faction and the European Arabs known today as Saracens proved too much for Basil to have a stable control of his Empire. So on the death of Ignatius, Photius was reconciled with Basil and once again was appointed by Basil to become the Patriarch of Constantinople and the personal tutor for Basil's son, Leo VI.

Let us continue to move a little further into history and come into the time of the next Byzantine ruler, Leo VI (886-912), the eldest son of the Emperor Basil I. One of his first acts upon succeeding his father was to depose his former teacher Photius from the Patriarchal in an attempt to secure the support of the uncompromising Patriarch of the Church (Hagia Sophia). During the reign of Leo VI the Byzantine Empire would continue to be physically threatened by European Arabs, and the Bulgarians or Bogomils of the Balkans. Both groups were Monophysites. Leo dealt with these threats with diplomacy rather than by military force. This strategy worked for the 24 years of his reign, which led Leo to make favorable concessions to both factions.

Take note of the fact that all Patriarchs of the Hagia Sophia were African Dyophysitic Christians, believing in the two natures of Christ. This differed from the African Patriarchs of Constantinople, Egypt, Syria and Ethiopia who were Monophysites, believing in the one nature of Christ, by declaring that Christ had an Osiris like spirit only, but no human nature. This feud went on for 921 years until the disciples and followers of the African Monist, Ibn Al-Arabi alias Muhammed, used his biography and the life that he lived to create Monist Muhammedanism in the middle of the thirteenth century. In the late 19th century and early 20th century, Arabi's life became the foundation for the traditional Muhammed of Islam.

Also take note of the fact that the Church of Hagia Sophia, the first seat of Dyophysitic Orthodox Christianity, lasted until 1453 when Muhammed II conquered Constantinople and seized the Church. And, subsequently, the seat (See) of Dyophysitic Christianity was transferred out of Africa to the suburbs of Rome (today's Vatican). In preparation for the imminent move, they had begun the building of Saint Peters Church over the catacombs or burial grounds in the year 1445.

The Vatican became the second See or seat for Christianity. For the first time in History, the Europeans living in Europe had total control of Christianity and the church without political interference thus began the separation of church and state. In 1445, Europeans began to practice their brand of Western (European) Christianity, giving the populace of the world the false illusion that the first seat (See) of Christianity was created and began in Europe.

Now I will provide you with a chronological list of

Byzantine Rulers of Constantinople. This was a particularly tumultuous period in history as the list reflects numerous rulers. Usurping and murder were the order of the day. The Byzantine Rulers struggled with the Saracen Monophysite non-Christian Arabs, Seljukian savage Turks, the Slavic Monophysitic Bogomils of the Balkans, the Christian Crusaders from Europe, and later the savage Ottoman Turks. All tried to penetrate the doubled walled city of Constantinople, take control of the Byzantine Empire, and seize the rich Church of Hagia Sophia.

Ironically, the Latin Emperors that are listed were invited to enter Constantinople by the Byzantine-ruling Emperors to become co-rulers, which lasted for 57 years in order to secure help from the West.

Rulers of the Byzantine Empire:

912 – 913	Alexander
913 – 919	Constantine VII
919 – 944	Romanus I
944 – 959	Constantine VII
959 – 963	Romanus II
963	Basil II
963 - 969	Nicephorus II (Phocas)
969 – 976	John I (Tz'mices)
976 – 1025	Basil II (restored)
1025 – 1028	Constantine VIII
1028 – 1034	Zoe and Romanus III
1034 – 1041	Zoe and Michael IV

1041 – 1042	Zoe and Michael V
1042 -	Zoe and Theodora
1042 – 1050	Zoe, Theodora, and Constantine IX
1055 – 1056?	Theodora
1056 – 1057	Michael VI
1057 – 1059	Isaac I Comnenus
1059 – 1067	Constantine X Ducas
1067 – 1068	Michael VII Ducas
1068 – 1071	Romanus IV (Diogenes)
1071 – 1078	Michael VII restored)
1078 – 1081	Nicephorus III (Botaniates)
1081 – 1118	Alexius I (Comnenus)
1118 – 1143	John II
1142 – 1180	Manuel I (Comnenus)
1180 – 1183	Alexius II (Comnenus)
1183 – 1185	Andronicus I (Comnenus)
1185 – 1195	Isaac II (Angelus)
1195 – 1203	Alexius III (Angelus)
1203 – 1204	Isaac II (restored)&Alexius IV
1204 -	Alexius V (Ducas)
1204 – 1222	Theodore I (lascarius (Nicaea, Empire of)
1222 – 1254	John III (Vatatzes or Ducas) (Nicaea)
1254 – 1258	Theodore II (Nicaea)
1259	Michael Palaeologus(Michael VIII)
1258 – 1261	John IV (Nicaea)
1261 – 1282	Michael VIII (recovered Constantinople from Baldwin)
1282 – 1338	Andronicus II

Latin Emperors or Co-Rulers of Constantinople:

1204 – 1205	Baldwin I
1205 – 1216	Henry VI
1216 – 1217	Peter de Courtenay
1218 – 1228	Robert de Courtenay
1228 – 1261	Baldwin II

In the next chapter, I will explain the true historical facts concerning the crusades that actually took place in Africa. This subject along with the other subjects that I have been writing about in this book are parts of the history that had to be revealed. It is crucial in order for the reader to understand how time, real people, real places, and actual events brought about the religion called Christianity and the religion that was first called Muhammedanism and later to be called Islam came into existence. It also gives some history of what happened to our African Ancient Egyptian ancestors after the Greeks invaded Egypt in 332 B.C.E.

CHAPTER IV

THE COMING OF THE CRUSADES IN AFRICA

In traditional literature written about the Crusades, it is said that a Pope by the name of Urban II first preached the formation of a crusade in 1095. This literature goes on to say that at the close of the Council of Clarmont Urban launched an appeal urging the Knights of France and Italy to cease fighting each other and go to the aid of the See and their brothers in the Christian east (Africa). Attacks of the Byzantine Emperors and their Empire by the Seljukian Turks were the reason for this call. The literature purports that Urban spoke of rescuing the Holy Sepulchre then under Turkish domination and his promise of full remission of sin to all joining the expedition, destination Jerusalem set as the goal. My research allows me to dispel the traditional literature written about the Crusades.

When the literature speaks of a Pope Urban II or a Church of the Holy Sepulchre, for example, the question must be asked, Pope of what Church? (1) There was no See (seat) for Christianity or a Vatican in Rome or in any other countries of Europe in 1095. The first and only See or seat of authority for Christianity at this time was in Northeast Africa, specifically the Church of Hagia Sophia in Constantinople, Turkey. (2) The building of the Church of St. Peter in 1445 marked the beginning of the Vatican being built in Rome and the first time the transfer of authority for Christianity to Europe. This was eight years prior to the imminent fall of Constantinople and the take over of the Hagia Sophia by the Ottoman Sultan Muhammed II in 1453 who took control of Constantinople, seized the Hagia Sophia and turned it into a mosque. Thus ending the Byzantine Empire and Era.

The Church of the Hagia Sophia did not have popes, with the exception of one individual, the African Melchite, Vigillus. He was the first official Pope or Papa from 537-553. Vigilius had full ecclesiastical authority over the church for the western world (Europeans) by the authority of the Donation of Constantine given to the Melchite African community by Constantine I to Sylvester I in 313-314. Vigilius retained ecclesiastical authority until it was taken from him by the Byzantine Emperor, Justinian I at the Council of Constantinople II in 553. When Justinian took back the Donation of Constantine, he gave himself full ecclesiastical authority to be added along with his political power over the Byzantine Empire and now the Church of Hagia Sophia. (See Chapter VII in the revised edition of *The Historical Origin of Christianity* by this Author). After taking back the Donation of Constantine, all ecclesiastical authority was in the hands of the Byzantine Emperor. This authority passed from emperor to emperor. The emperor was the only one who had the authority to appoint the Patriarch (Bishop) of the Hagia Sophia and the Monophysite Patriarch of

Constantinople. Again, the Church of Hagia Sophia being the first and only See or Seat for Christianity during the Byzantine Era did not have popes, only Patriarchs appointed by the Byzantine Emperor.

The existence of a Church of the Holy Sepulchre in 1095 is another fallacy. It is written in today's traditional history that according to the writings of one Eusebius Pamphili, a.k.a., Eusebius of Caesarea (260?-340?) he is said to have written a history of the early church, the life of Constantine, and ten volumes of ecclesiastical theological treatises. He is also listed in today's history books as a Greek historian, bishop, one of the Fathers of the early church, and a church historian. He is said to have written that Constantine ordered the building of the Church of the Holy Sepulchre known also as the Church of the Resurrection. In the supposed writings of Eusebius, it is stated that Constantine is said to have thought it was his duty to establish a structure that would serve as a subject of universal admiration at the place of the savior's resurrection in Jerusalem. And, therefore, he was prompted to order a house of worship to be built (326-335 A.B.C.E.). The tale goes on to say that Constantine's mother, Helena, now known today as St. Helena founded the true cross at this site. Now with all this being said, let me bring forth the facts repudiating this fallacy. I will start with the incarnated name of Eusebius. In traditional literature, it is stated that Eusebius was a 4th century church historian and father of the Church.

Note: The phrase "The Church" refers to the Roman Catholic Church in Rome.

History does not support a Christ in the 4th century. The name or title Christ or (K)Christos was first given to the icon Serapis who was anointed (K)Christos at the Council of Ephesus in 431 A.B.C.E., which is the 5th century, thereby, creating a title and object for Christianity. Secondly, Christianity as a religion officially began at the close of the Council of Chalcedon in 451 A.B.C.E. also the 5th century. Thirdly, the world's first Christian Church, the Hagia Sophia was built in Constantinople, Turkey in Northeast Africa (532 A.C.E. and finished in 537 A.C.E.) by the Byzantine Emperor, Justinian and his wife Theodora. And the fourth reason, the supposed "Holy Land" or Holy City in Jerusalem where the Church of the Holy Sepulchre is located today is only a few years over a hundred years old. (See the documentary film by E. Sax, "The Jerusalem Syndrome." Therefore, there was no "Holy Land" in the 4th century in Jerusalem. With the aforementioned reasons being fully understood, one can now see why it is not possible to have Eusebius, Christ, Christianity, or a Christian Church in the 4th Century.

FIRST CRUSADE

Contrary to common presumption, it is very important to understand that all the Crusades took place in Northeast Africa and did not take place in Europe. Let's begin with the Seljukian Turks who invaded Turkey and the Byzantine Empire via Iran in 1071. Ten years after the Turkish invasion the Byzantine Emperors realized that they could not defeat the Seljukian Turks with their regular army. So they began to hire knights from Europe to serve as mercenaries to add more manpower to protect their Empire, the capital city of Constantinople, and the Church of Hagia Sophia. Alexius I (Comnenus) was the Byzantine Emperor during this time period from, 1081-1118. However, before going on, it is important for the reader to be reminded of some facts about the first crusade.

I reiterate the fact that Urban II, identified as a Pope, and his supposed speech at Clermont in 1095 is no more than a decoy to steer you from certain facts concerning the crusade that took place in actual world history in Africa. Let's begin with the call from Emperor Alexius I who in 1096 asked the Barons in the West (France, Italy, and Germany) for help in stopping the attacks on the Empire by the Seljukian Turks. Tradition says that two persons responded after hearing Urban II's call, one was Peter the Hermit, a French preacher, and the other was the knight, Walter the Penniless, who led a group from Germany. They left for Jerusalem in the spring of 1096 under the pretense of defending the Holy Sepulchre and Christendom. Peter and Walter and their bands have been described as undisciplined and unorganized thugs seeking personal gain and glory. In any case human history does not support an Urban II as a Pope.

A more credible scenario is that Urban was a preacher or bishop in France under the jurisdiction of the Patriarch of the Hagia Sophia who had been appointed by the Emperor Alexius I. By all accounts, he was an ambitious politician and opportunist. It is probable that once Urban received the call from Alexius, he informed Peter the Hermit and Walter the Penniless before he apprised the Barons of the request. This gave Urban an opportunity to devise his scheme, have the land surveyed, and take whatever land and riches they could take for him and themselves, and perhaps, destroy the city of Constantinople and the Seat of Christianity (Hagia Sophia) itself. Politicians are known for deal making. Urban could have had his ambitious sites set on a See in France. If the See in Africa had fallen immediately, it is likely that the new See would have been in France (Europe) with Urban as the Vicar of Christ (Pope).

Their goals were not realized and both suffered defeat, Peter the Hermit in Turkey by the Seljuks and Walter the Penniless in the Balkans by the Bogomils. After Walter's encounter with the Bogomils in the Balkans, he reached Constantinople with less than a hundred haggard men. Peter the Hermit and his few remaining followers reached Constantinople prior to Walter and his group. In January

1097, some survivors from each group along with Peter and Walter joined up with the Army of the Barons (Lombards), those for whom the call from Alexius was originally intended.

The armies of the Barons consisted of four groups. Godfrey of Bouillon and his brother Baldwin from the North of France commanded the first army. The second army was commanded by Raymond of Toulouse, which originated in the South of France. The third was under the command of Stephen of Blois and Robert of Normandy. They marched from Central France. The fourth came from Southern Italy with Bohemund of Toranto commanding. In the spring of 1097, they all assembled in Constantinople before the Emperor Alexius Comnenus who obtained from each leader an oath of peace and a promise to restore to the Byzantine Empire territories that they might take from the Turks. This pact was never honored during the history of the Crusades. Instead, the Barons seized this opportunity to acquire land in order to expand their personal land holdings and to expand trade. Antioch fell after a long fought battle with the Turks in 1098. Jerusalem fell after a short battle in 1099. These areas, however, were not handed over to the Byzantine Emperor as sworn, but became the center of the Crusader states in the Levant or land areas of Northeast Africa.

Constantinople was spared. However, the fall of Constantinople was viewed as imminent given that it was as an island surrounded by a sea of Monophysites or quasi-Christians. In the meantime, the Crusaders who were assembled in Northeast Africa were joined by contingents coming in by sea. From Northwestern Italy came the Genoese in 1098 and from the same area of Italy came the Pisans in 1099. Later, came the Venetians from Northeastern Italy and the Norwegians from Norway. They all helped to maintain control of the land areas taken by the armies of the Barons. But the Burgundians of Eastern France, Germany, and a large group of Christian **Knights** from other parts of Europe, who had left at the news of the fall of Jerusalem to Godfrey and Baldwin, were annihilated by the Turks while crossing Asia Minor (Turkey) in 1101.

SECOND CRUSADE

When news arrived of the capture of Edessa by the Turks in 1144, a supposed Pope Eugene III organized a Second Crusade according to traditional historical literature. However, I am saying the same things about this Pope Eugene III that I said about the supposed Urban II in the beginning of this chapter. Louis VII of France and Conrad III of Germany organized this second crusading call in response to the appeal of Bernard of Clairvaux. Both took the land route along the Danube, passed through Constantinople, but acted separately in joining battle with the Turks across Asia Minor.

Conrad III and Louis VII both suffered extremely

heavy casualties at the hands of the Turks and had to flee Asia Minor for their lives. At the same time an army of French and English Crusaders came to Asia Minor by sea to help in the fight against the Turks. They took part in an attack on Damascus that failed in 1148. At that point they returned to their ships. By then it became steadily clearer that the Latin States in Northeast Africa were in danger. After these failed attempts several or more calls for a crusade were made with little or no success (1165-1169). These appeals were renewed more urgently after 1181, which also had no effect. Then in 1187 Saladin the Turk took the crusading Barons main prize possession, Jerusalem. And thus set in motion the third crusade from 1188-1192.   By this time, the Byzantine Emperors realized that the armies of the Barons and other crusading forces were not fighting the Turks to protect their Empire or the seat of Christianity (Hagia Sophia) from being destroyed. But were crusading for their own personal gain, which was to acquire more land ownership. This was even more evident when the Barons' armies conquered Edessa, Nicaea, and Jerusalem and kept and claimed these areas for their personal kingdoms, establishing what is known today in history as the Latin States.

THIRD CRUSADE

The Third Crusade brought on the German Emperor Frederick I Barbarossa who followed the Danube and crossed into Byzantine territory despite the hostility of the Byzantine Emperor who knew that these supposed crusaders were looking for personal gain and not to save the Byzantine Empire or Christendom. However, Frederick I met his demise by drowning in a river while crossing hostile Turkish territory. Taking up the call after the demise of Frederick I was King Phillip II or Augusta of France and Richard I the Lion of England. Both left by sea to join other crusaders who were scattered throughout Asia Minor and the areas outside of Jerusalem. Richard had conquered the Island of Cyprus from the Byzantine Emperor Isaac II Angelus and then went on to seize Acre. After a long fought battle, Richard reoccupied several coastal sites of Jaffa and Ascalon, but did not dare attack Jerusalem, which was occupied by Saladin the Turk.

FOURTH CRUSADE

Five years later an expedition was organized by Barbarossa's son, Henry VI, which is called the German Crusade from 1197-1198. This crusade had no success because Henry died before embarking on his journey to join the other crusaders, already in Northeast Africa. The news of his death caused the crusaders who had sailed in advance of Henry to return to the West (Europe). In the interim, crusade preaching started up again in 1198 when the nobility of the county of Champagne, France took the call in response to the urging of Fulk of Neuilly. Some Italian Barons joined the French, commanded by Boniface DeMontferrat who decided to go by sea. This expedition hit a snag. When the knights came to embark, they could not pay the sum promised to the shipowners and were forced to discharge their debt by helping the Venetians take the city of Zara from the King of Hungary.

Note: In order for you the reader of this book to understand the man-created religion called Islam, it was necessary to walk you through 921 years of Byzantine history, Monophysite history and the Crusades in order to get to the time of Ibn Al 'Arabi alias Muhammed.

Continuing with the crusades, we come to the time of Alexius IV who was the brother-in-law of the German King Phillip of Swabia. Alexius promised to join the crusade and divide the Empire if the army would help him usurp the throne of Byzantium. After the promise was made, the crusaders began the expedition that reached Constantinople in 1203. The army helped Alexius to usurp the throne of Isaac II who had just been restored to the throne after usurping Alexius III Angelus. However, Alexius IV was not able to keep his promise because Alexius V Ducas usurped him. This left the Crusaders encamped around the double walls of Constantinople. After running out of food and other resources, they decided to assault the Byzantine capital and divide the city among themselves. Storming the city, the soldiers looted and destroyed for three days with neither order nor discipline. And as a result, Constantinople and the Empire never fully recovered from this treatment. On May 16, 1204, Count Baldwin of Flanders, France was crowned Latin Emperor of Constantinople.

The Count of Flanders became Baldwin I, the first Latin King or co-ruler of Constantinople. Eight years later in 1212 a popular movement was triggered in France and Germany that was called The Children's Crusade. This Crusade was to be made part of The Fourth Crusade. A young undisciplined and unorganized group of teenagers and young adults without weapons, leadership, or resources tried to initiate a crusade of their own, but this so-called crusade fizzled before they could leave France. Much later it was reported that merchants of Marseilles had transported hundreds to Egypt, where they were sold as slaves.

FIFTH CRUSADE

This brings us to the Fifth Crusade that was called in 1213 and commenced in 1217 when King Andrew II of Hungary, Duke Leopold VI of Austria and John of Brienne were among the leaders of the expedition that was aimed at Jerusalem and Egypt. King Andrew and the Duke of Austria landed in Jerusalem in 1217 only to be defeated by the Turks who had full control of Jerusalem. After their departure John of Brienne decided to carry the war into Egypt in 1218. Egypt was the center of Turkish Monophysite strength and power. With the arrival of more crusaders, this enabled John to take control of Damietta in 1219. The attack caused the Sultan of Egypt to make an offer to John that he would give back Jerusalem to the crusaders in return for Damietta. John did not accept the offer, but instead decided to continue the conquest of Egypt by marching on Cairo that ended in his defeat. The crusaders escaped captivity only by surrendering Damietta back to the Turks in 1221.

SIXTH CRUSADE

Two years later, Frederick II, Holy Roman Emperor of Germany, was pressured by the Christians of France to agree on an expedition in Northeast Africa. A sixth crusade was launched in 1223. This crusade is often referred to as the Bloodless Crusade. As a result, Frederick was despised and called a traitor and non-believer by the Christians in the West (Europe). Subsequently, the Christian community of Europe excommunicated him. Frederick was a peacemaker and lover of intellectual subjects such as poetry, religious philosophy and other intellectual thoughts rather than war. He was a bridge between war and religious philosophy. Frederick also is credited with the founding of a private school in Naples. He was King of Germany and the two Sicilies. Later he would become the Latin King of Jerusalem located in the area of Jerusalem occupied by the Knights Templars who were soldiers in Godfrey's army and who had settled there after 1099 following the conquest by Godfrey of Bouillon and his brother Baldwin. Obviously, there was an understanding between the Knights Templars and the Turks. The Templars were Dhimmi's or taxpayers who paid the Turks to stay in Jerusalem and agreed not to wage war against them. They were able to pay their way easily given their personal association with the rich Lombards or Barons of Europe. The harmony and tolerance between the Knight Templars and the Turks lasted until the Mamelukes ran them out in 1291. Let's go back to Frederick, the Holy Roman Emperor.

Frederick's tolerance of religious differences was a major influence and had a great impact with the Turks. He was an unusual personality of the times. Frederick was an educated man whose background was of mixed parents. He, therefore, was able to show a tolerance for not only a diversity of people, but also a diversity of beliefs and reflected this tolerance in his policies. Being a contemporary of the intellectual mystic Arabi and visiting in and around the same land area where Arabi lived, it is probable that Frederick II himself met Arabi in Africa and was an admirer. Arabi was very popular among the African and European Monophysites and understood their thoughts on religious ideology. Frederick was empathetic to the Monophysitic way of thinking, towards Dyophysitic Christianity, and the Christ image. This surely infuriated the European Christian community in Europe especially in France. With Frederick having political authority over the Christians in France, Innocent IV gathered a group of European theologians together to convoke a council meeting in France in 1245, which is known in history as the First Ecumenical Council of Lyons. During this time, I can safely state that the European Christian community had minimal contact with Constantinople and the Church of Hagia Sophia due to the fighting and turmoil created by the Crusaders, Turks, and the usurping of the leadership of the Byzantine Emperors.

At the Council of Lyons Innocent IV wanted to defuse the ecclesiastical authority of Frederick. They were successful in excommunicating Frederick. And, it is highly probable that they most likely voted for the next See (seat) of Christianity to be in Paris, France. Their sights most likely were set on the newly finished Church of Notre Dame in Paris that was completed in 1230. However, this did not occur at this time in history. The moving of the See of Christianity from Africa (Constantinople via the Church of Hagia Sophia) to Europe would not occur for two hundred years after the first Council of Lyons I (1245).

The next major building project in Europe would occur on the outskirts of Rome over the catacombs. They began to build St. Peters Church, the new See (Seat) for Christianity, in 1445 with Eugenius IV leading the way.

St. Peters became the cornerstone building of what is now Vatican City. This is where the Europeans began to practice Western (European) Christianity, thereby erasing the Coptic Egyptian origin of this religion, which gave the world a totally European worldview of Christianity. The hierarchy began to elect their own Popes, thereby, creating their own papacy without political or government interference. Church and State separated. The Sixth Crusade was viewed as a romantic victory. It was during the time of Frederick that Arabi enjoyed the height of his popularity and his fame was widely known among the African and European Monophysites in Africa. Arabi taught and propounded his monistic views on God, spirituality, Prophethood, and Sufi ideology, which began to change the African and European Monophysites' way of thinking. In the next chapter, I will raise questions about Mecca and Medina.

CHAPTER V

COMMENTS AND QUESTIONS ABOUT MECCA and MEDINA OUTSIDE OF ISLAMIC TRADITION

Before commencing with this chapter, I would like to remind you once again what the *Shorter Encyclopedia of Islam* has to say about the traditional Prophet Muhammed of Islam. It states, "in consequence of the unreliability of the sources at our disposal, the very first question a biographer has to ask, namely when was his hero born, cannot be answered with certainty." The hero in this quote refers to the traditional object of Islam, the created creature Muhammed the Prophet. Another quote from Shorter states, "that Muhammed's activity in Medina covered ten years (622-632) is certain; but we have no certain data for the Meccan period."

♦ Comment: Without a biography of a supposed person as spoke of in traditional Islam ever walking the earth in human form, you cannot have the hero of Islamic tradition, Muhammed." Also, without having specific data for the Meccan period, you cannot have a Muhammed being born in Mecca (570) or buried in Medina after death in 632.

♦ Comment: I want to remind the reader that in the study of Byzantine history and era (330-1453) there is no mention of a Prophet Muhammed, Islam, or Muslims. Instead you will find arguments between the Coptic African Monophysites and the Coptic African

Dyophysitic Christians over the human nature of Christ and later physical violence by the European Arab Monophysites against the Byzantine government and empire. Let's go into another glaring discrepancy. Neither Mecca or Medina existed under those names as places in physical or geographical form where Hajj or pilgrimages were being held and conducted before the rule and control of Arabia and the Hejaz by Abdul Aziz AL Saud in 1924. More will be said on Abdul Aziz AL Saud as we proceed in this chapter. At this point, let's continue with the reasons as to why there was no physical Mecca or a religious Hajj before 1926 when the first meeting in Islam history first occurred.

About Mecca

In the *Encyclopedia Britannica 15th edition*, in the article on Mecca states, "Ancient Mecca was an oasis on the old caravan trade route that linked the Mediterranean world with South Arabia, East Africa, and South Asia. Located about midway between Ma'rib in the South and Petra in the North, the town gradually developed during Roman and Byzantine times into an important trade and religious center. It was known to Ptolemy as Macoraba....During biblical times, the city was ruled by a series of Yemeni tribes. Under the Quraysh, it became a type of city-state, with strong commercial links to the rest of Arabia, Ethiopia, and Europe. Mecca became a place for trade for pilgrimage, and for poetry festivals."

Facts, Comments, and Questions

♦ To what Ptolemy is this article referring? There were fourteen Ptolemy Greek Rulers of Egypt starting with the founder of the Dynasty, Ptolemy I Lagi called Soter (Savior). Ptolemy Lagi was the one who succeeded Alexander the Greek and became ruler of Egypt after his death in 323 BCE. The title "Ptolemy" means Greek Ruler of Egypt. So again, I ask which Ptolemy? Or, was it the pseudo Claudius Ptolemy listed in Western academia and literature as an astronomer and geographer (about 100-170 A.D.)?

Note: Everything that you have read in the aforementioned Encyclopedia *Britannica* article is based on Islamic tradition and not true human historical facts.

♦ Muslims maintain that "Mecca is the Holy City of Islam and the birthplace of Muhammed." According to the Quran, "the first sanctuary appointed for mankind was that at Bakkah (or Mecca), a blessed place, a guidance for the peoples" (Sura 3:96). In Sura 6:92 and 42:5, we find that Mecca is the "Mother of all settlements." Also, according to Islamic tradition, Adam placed the Black stone in the original Kaaba there, while Abraham and Ishmael rebuilt the Kaaba many years later. Thus, by traditional implication, Mecca is considered by the Islamic world to be the first and most important city in the world! Let me remind you once again of what the *Shorter Encyclopedia of Islam* says about this created creature Muhammed the Prophet of Islam, "Muhammed's activity in Medina covered 10 years (622-632) is certain. But we have no certain data for the Meccan period."

♦ Comment: The foundation of Islam depends upon a Muhammed being born in Mecca in 570 A.D. Therefore, after reading the above quote, this leaves the traditional teaching of Muhammed being born in Mecca in doubt.

Allow me to elaborate on this mythical story a bit more. Again, according to Islamic belief and traditions when Adam and Eve were cast forth from paradise, they fell in different parts of the earth. Adam fell on a mountain on the Island of Serendip, or Sri Lanka, and Eve fell in Arabia, on the border of the Red Sea near the present port of Jidda/Jeddah. For two hundred years they wandered separately and lonely about the earth. Finally, in consideration of their penitence and wretchedness, they were permitted to come together again on Mt. Arafat, near the present city of Mecca. Adam prayed to God that a shrine might be granted to him one similar to what he used for worship in paradise. Adam's prayers were answered and a shrine was built. This shrine supposedly passed away, and many generations later, Abraham and his son Ishmael rebuilt the ancient tabernacle. Gabriel assisted them and brought a magic stone for the shrine (some believers speculate that this stone was a meteorite). The shrine was called the Ka'bah and the supposed Abrahamic Haggarian pilgrimage to it called the Hajj began.

♦ Comment: Remember that the Adam and Eve story comes from Genesis in the Old Testament. The Old Testament, Psalms, and the Four Gospels of the New Testament were used to create the Koran and Islam by Jewish scholars and Rabbis from the Alliance Israelite Universaille of Paris, France. Beginning in 1870 in Syria along with the help of Christian and Arab scholars who helped in the creation of the Koran and Islam. The Jewish scholars and Rabbis also added in the mix Sefer Ha Yashar literature that are called the "Books of the Upright Ones," i.e., Abraham, Isaac, Jacob, and Moses. The books, Sefer Ha Yashar (Torah) became the basic foundation for the Torah and Talmud, and the religion today known as Judaism. It was Moses Maimon or Maimonides, inspired by the literary writings of RASHI, who first created the Old Testament or Pentateuch in 1168-1180 A.C.E. It was printed first in 1475 by the Capitalist press for the Christian world community in Bologna, Italy.

Note: These biblical stories come 610 years after the traditional 570 A.C.E. birth date of Muhammed the Prophet of Islam.

If you are one to believe in the traditional teaching that Judaism was the first western religion before Christianity and Monophysite Christianity, you have been misinformed historically. The historically correct order is Christianity first and then Monophysitic Christianity second from which Monist Muhammedanism derived, and then Judaism/Islam (third). Remember that Judaism is not a B.C. religion for it cannot predate Solomon bar Isaac called RASHI (1040-1104), its creator and formulator whose writings inspired Maimonides. Neither can Judaism predate the first Crusade of 1096. In simple language the world had no religion called Judaism before the French baron RASHI, Moses Maimonides, Jacob ben Meir, or the Knights Templars. They all played a hand in the creation and development of Judaism.

Islam is a religion that was created by Jewish scholars using the old and the New Testament writings to create the Koran, Islam, and Israelite tales or Isra'iliyat to help create the Prophet Muhammed of tradition.

◆ Comment: It was IBN Al'Arabi who first created the ritual of going on a Hajj or pilgrimage to Mecca, an imaginary mental state. This ritual created by Arabi caused him to go around in a circle while chanting prayers and casting out stones to rid one self of personal sins. Mecca originally was a state of mind only for the many followers and disciples of Arabi based on one's imagination, faith, belief, and the teachings of Ibn Al 'Arabi alias Muhammed. His teachings became part of Islamic tradition. Proof of this fact is that millions of modern Muslims visit Mecca every day through the act of praying. Some pray five times each day. Throughout the vast Muhammedan/Islamic Arab world, millions upon millions of believers kneel to pray. Wherever the place of prayer, they face towards Mecca and are united to the Kaaba by an invisible imaginary line of direction called the (K) Qibla.

♦ Questions: If Mecca is supposed to be the birthplace of the Prophet Muhammed (570ACE), thereby, making Mecca a supposed Holy City, I ask the question again, why was Mecca called Macoraba during the Byzantine era and not called Mecca? Again I want to bring out the fact that if you study Byzantine History (395-1453) or Ottoman Turkish history (1300-1919); you will find no mention of Mecca, Medina, or a Prophet Muhammed. The question, when did Mecca become a physical Holy City for the Islamic world for the first time in world history?

♦ Answer: After the fall of the Ottoman Empire (1919) and the forming of the League of Nations (1920), the League of Nations gave the British and the French in 1920-1921 land regions in Northeast Africa. Today the region is referred to as the Middle East, such as Turkey, Syria, Lebanon, Jordan, Palestine, Iraq, Kuwait, Iran, Arabia, and Yemen through a mandate. The British and the French began to issue these land areas to their hand picked puppets. For example, Abdullah, the son of Sherif Hussein as Emir in Jordan, Faisal another son of Sherif Hussein was made Emir of Iraq after it was bordered off from Arabia in 1921by the British under their mandate.

This was done because in 1916 Sherif Hussein Ibn Ali and his son Faisal with the help of the British and their agent, T.E. Lawrence, a.k.a., Lawrence of Arabia destroyed Turkish control of the Hejaz province in Arabia, Iran, where Mecca and Medinah are located today. After the fall of the Turkish Empire (1919) Arabia was up for grabs. The British backed Abdul Aziz Al-Saud who defeated Sherif Hussein Ibn Ali for control of Araby (Arabia) in 1924. More will be said on this as you read further. However, let me continue to comment concerning Mecca.

♦ Comment: There is no mention of Mecca or the Kaaba in any authenticated Ancient documents including the Vatican archives. <u>Mecca is dated by Islamic tradition by using the phrase "according to the Quran".</u>

♦ According to extensive research done by Richard Bulliet, a historian who wrote on the history of trade in the ancient Middle East, he said "these claims by Muslims are quite wrong, as Mecca simply was not on the major trading routes." The reason for this he contends is that "Mecca is tucked away at the edge of the Peninsula. Only by the most tortured reading can it be described as a natural crossroads between a North-South route and an East-West one," i.e., the land region where Mecca is today was a very difficult and out of the way place to reach. Additionally, Mecca is said to have been very rugged and undesirable.

♦ Comment: With all of this being said, how could it have been a place to have Hajj or pilgrimages?

Patricia Crone in her work entitled, *Meccan Trade and the Rise of Islam,* also adds a practical reason that is too often overlooked by earlier historians. She points out that "Mecca was a barren place, and barren places do not make natural halts, and least of all when they are found at a short distance from famously green environments. Why should caravans have made a steep descent to the barren valley of Mecca when they could have stopped at Ta'if?" This is a region in the Arabian Hejaz 75 miles east of Mecca. Or if I the author may ask, why not the seaport region of Jidda, a city on the eastern shores of the Red Sea which today ranks as Saudi Arabia's second largest city. Jidda also is a region in the Hejaz that was used for trade and commerce. However, it was not developed as a city until 1934. Jidda today serves as the gateway to the Moslem Holy cities of Mecca and Medina. Today Moslem pilgrims from throughout the world pass through Jidda on their sacred journey to reach Mecca and Medina.

♦ Comment: Ta'if had water and food supplies, whereby Mecca was rugged, barren and hilly, and without food or water supplies plus it was very difficult to access.

Further, Patricia Crone asks, "What commodity was available in Arabia that could be transported such a distance, through such an inhospitable environment and still be sold at a profit large enough to support the growth of a city in a peripheral site bereft of natural resources?"

♦ Comment: Further, I would like to say that prior to calling the first meeting in Islam's history in 1926 Abdul Aziz Al-Saud began a campaign to suppress the robbing and extortion in the Meccan region. I will share information regarding that meeting with you as you read further.

Crone concludes this discussion in her work by pointing out that Greek trading documents refer to Ta'if, and to Yathrib (today called Medina), as well as Kaybar in the North, but no mention is made of Mecca.

♦ Comment: If Mecca was so important, certainly those to whom the trade was being done would have noted its existence, yet, there is no records of trade with Mecca to be found.

I will now share with you the first meeting in Islam's history, which will continue to prove that there was no Hajj or pilgrimages taking place in today's Mecca before Abdul Aziz-Al Saud gained control of Arabia in 1924. The following will explain the reason why the first meeting in Islam's history was called, followed by the speech that was read on behalf of HM (His Majesty) King

Abdul Aziz-Al Saud, founder of the kingdom of Arabia, today Saudi Arabia. I will quote from the book, *The Holy Quran and the Sword Selected Addresses, Speeches, Memoranda, and Interviews*, by HM, the late King Abdul Aziz-Al Saud.

FIRST MEETING IN ISLAM'S HISTORY

"Immediately after Mustafa Kamal (Ataturk) had abolished the Turkey-based Islamic Caliphate (1343H-1924G), turmoil reigned supreme in the Muslim world, with many countries calling for the continuation of the Caliphate and pledging allegiance to a new Caliph. Delegations from many Islamic countries came in droves to discuss the situation with HM (His Majesty) King Abdul Aziz. They were entertaining the hope that allegiance would be pledged to HM as Caliph, being the only one among Muslim Kings, Sultans, Emirs, and Rulers, who was qualified for the Caliphate and enjoyed the Caliph qualities prescribed by the canon law of Islam or Sharia. HM declined the offer, giving the delegations his objective justification. HM's approach encapsulated in that a Muslim Caliph's decision must be enforced by all Muslim countries. But, as most of these countries are under foreign colonial powers, the restoration of the Caliphate will be a vein, formal act which HM cannot approve of. At the time, King Faud of Egypt spearheaded Arab rulers who feverishly sought the title of Caliph. Lacking qualities prescribed by Sharia and with his country under foreign domination, even Egyptian Muslim scholars rejected his attempt. When King Faud called for convening an Islamic conference-ostensibly to discuss the restoration of Islamic Caliphate, but actually to pledge allegiance to him as Caliph-few countries responded and the conference failed. Amidst this perplexity, HM King Abdul Aziz called for convening an Islamic conference in Mecca Al – Mukarrammah. The Caliphate issue was not on the agenda of the conference, which was to discuss means of unifying Muslim ranks and a host of Islamic issues. Attended by many Muslim countries including Egypt, the conference was opened on the 20th of Dhul quadiah 1344H (3 March 1926G). The following speech was read on behalf of HM King Abdul Azizi:

'Praise be to Allah, who hath guided us to this (felicity): never could we have found guidance, had it not been for the guidance of Allah.' Peace and blessings be upon Prophet Muhammed, the Messenger of Allah, his companions, and those who followed his righteous path. I welcome and thank you for favorably responding to the call for convening this conference. Dear ardent Muslims, In form and substance, this meeting may be the first of its kind in Islam's history. We beseech Allah that it will be a good precedent, hoping that it will be repeated every year complying with the Koranic verse: "Help ye one another in righteousness and piety, but help ye not one another in sin and rancor." Another Koranic verse said: "And take mutual council together, according to what is just and reasonable." During past eras, little attention was given to what is known today as Islamic public opinion or local public opinion, to which rulers may revert for consultations, with regard to required reform in the cradle of Islam, where-from it spread to all humanity. The Hijaz has been ruled by many states. Some of their Caliphs and Sultans paid attention to its affairs, and some –due to ignorance-inflicted harm, despite intentions. A third category paid no heed at all, leaving matters in the hands of their deputies. When matters reached a critical juncture and the Ulema (men who are the custodians of the tradition of Islam) decided that, according to Sharia, the cradle of Islam must be saved, we rushed to the rescue. Relying on Allah Almighty, we strove with our belongings and person in the cause of Allah. With Allah's support, we cleansed the Holy Land, fulfilling our pledge to Allah and our promise to Muslims. The promises we started to implement included a call for convening an Islamic conference. The letters containing invitation for the conference explained our personal plan and views. When the state of war ended with the reins of government placed into our hands, wise men in Hijaz were of the opinion that it was not in their interest to wait for the convening of an Islamic conference. They were not sure that the conference would be held. Moreover, they doubted that the attendants would know their interests better than them. The delegation they dispatched to us explained that the interest of their country lies in preserving its internationally recognized independence under royal rule, pledging allegiance to us. Initially, we declined their offer. But, at the urging of the Ulema of Nejd, I accepted their oath of allegiance. Being no tyrannical rulers, we, the Saud Dynasty, abound by Sharia provisions and the decisions of Ulema. The personal call for convening the conference does not justify my disagreement with them. And, if I disagree with them without an acceptable justification according to Sharia, they will not obey me. The resulting mischief is distinctly evident. I have been pledged allegiance by Urbans and Chiefs of Bedouin tribes; the latter are decision-makers, as their tribes follow them in war and peace. However, I believe accepting the oath of allegiance and working with the citizens according to it rather than conquest and power, does not preclude benefiting from the views of Ulema and wise men in the Islamic world. Consequently, I have addressed the invitation for convening this conference giving it an all-encompassing theme."

Dear Brothers,
You have seen for yourselves and heard from those who came here for Hajj that security in the Hijaz- and between the two holy mosques-is being maintained at a degree of perfection unmatched for many centuries and even unrivaled in any of the world's most organized and powerful countries. Enjoying this security and freedom, governed only by Sharia provisions, I urge you to conduct consultations on interests and systems you deem acceptable to the Muslim world, establishing Islamic Sharia and abiding by its provisions.

Dear Conferees,

You are free at this conference. The government of this country places no restrictions beyond those stipulated by your religion, namely, adherence to its provisions. The only exception is that you should not indulge in international politics or disputes between some Islamic peoples and governments, as these matters only concern these peoples. Muslims have been overwhelmed by sectarian differences. So, you should strive to narrow these differences and cooperate to achieve their common interests, ensuring that different schools of thought and races should not lead to animosity: "And, hold fast, all together, by the rope which Allah stretches out to you, and be not divided among yourselves: and remember with gratitude Allah's favor on you: For ye were enemies and he joined your hearts in love, so that by his grace, ye become brethren: And, ye were on the brink of the pit of fire, and he saved you from it. Thus, does Allah make his signs clear let there arise out of you a band of people inviting to all that is good, enjoying what is right, and forbidding what is wrong: They are the ones to attain felicity. Be not like those who are divided among themselves and fall into disputations after receiving clear signs: For them is a dreadful chastisement."

♦ Comments: If according to tradition the religion known as Islam was revealed and given to the Prophet Muhammed by God through the angel Gabriel thus producing Islam (622-632), the question has to be asked: If the religion called Islam was produced at that time in world history, why did the Islamic world wait for over 1300 years to have its first meeting in Islam's history in 1926? This was not only the first meeting in Islam's history, but also the first physical Hajj or pilgrimage in Islam's history. This too was the first time in Islam's history to elect a Caliph as the leader for the Islamic world community. Note that there was no Ka'bah building representing the Ka'bah shrine/Mosque as it is today. At this meeting the Muslims prayed in an open area that was designated a Mosque.

♦ Comment: Abdul Aziz beginning in 1924 started the development and building of Mecca and Medina for the Islamic world to have their Hajj/Pilgrimage in physical form. This building/development has continued through the years. In the next chapter, more will be said on how Ibn Al 'Arabi's Monist views were developed into a new religion for the European Arab and African communities. Additionally in the next chapter I will introduce you to the man whose life and biography were used to create the traditional Prophet Muhammed of Islam, Shaikh Al Akbar Muhiyuddin Al 'Ali, a.k.a. Ibn Al 'Arabi alias Muhammed.

CHAPTER VI

WHO WAS SHAIKH AL 'AKBAR MUHIYUDDIN IBN AL 'ALI A.K.A. IBN AL 'ARABI, Alias MUHAMMED?

In this chapter I have confined myself to an overview biography of Ibn Al 'Arabi with a short account of his life, works, sayings, opinions of others, and his views in brief on a few topics. This is done with the help of Moulavi S.A.Q. Husaini, M.A. who translated some of Ibn Al 'Arabi's works in order to introduce Ibn Al 'Arabi to the English speaking world.

I will comment on things that need commenting on. So the question is who was The Shaikh Al Akbar Muhiyuddin Ibn Al Ali A.K.A. Ibn Al 'Arabi alias Muhammed. Let me introduce you to the biography of the person whose life was made into a Prophet by his disciples and followers in the mid-thirteenth century. Jewish Scholars collaborating with Christian and Arab Scholars in the latter part of the nineteenth century and early twentieth century participated in constructing Islam and the Koran. Thereby, creating the Prophet Muhammed of tradition.

LIFE AND TIMES OF IBN AL 'ARABI

First, let's clarify the confusion in history that exists

surrounding the identity of the Moors in Spain. Following on the heels of the invasion of Egypt by Alexander, the Greek in 332 B.C.E, Europeans out of Greece, the Balkans, and Southern Russia began settling in North and Northeast Africa in the fourth century B.C. The descendants of these European people later are identified in history as Saracens, now called Arabs, Muslims, and Moors. In 1051 the real Moors who were African Egyptian Monophysites and descendants of the Ancient Egyptians entered Spain. They were highly skilled and educated men and women who began to develop Spain by building cities such as Cordoba, Seville, Toledo, Granada and other areas throughout Spain, thus bringing a higher civilization to barbaric Spain. The credit for doing this is given to the European Saracen Arab, who is given the name Moor in today's history books. Instead, the credit for achieving and accomplishing these great fetes should be given to the African Coptic Egyptian Moors. The question is asked what is a Moor? The answer, a Moor is a person coming from North Africa (Mauritania or Morocco) crossing the Mediterranean Sea and entering Spain thereby, causing today's history books to overreach and call the barbaric European invaders "Moors."
Thereby, causing the people of the world to think that the high civilization that was brought to Spain was brought by the European Saracen Arabs, and thus erasing the legitimate indigenous African heirs of their credit and confusing the name Moor.

Shaikh Al 'Akbar Muhiyuddin Ibn Al 'Ali a.k.a. Ibn Al 'Arabi, alias Muhammed, was an African who was born in Spain on the night of 560 A.H. (July 29, 1165) in the city of Mursya (Murcia). This was a city of beautiful parks and gardens developed by the African Moors.

The Ancestors of Ibn Al 'Arabi had settled in Spain many years before his birth whereby, his father Ali became a Carpenter and lived in Seville until 597 A.H. (1202). Note what appears to be a coincidence. The name Ali in the traditional teaching of Islam is stated to be a cousin and son-in-law of Muhammed of tradition. Ibn Al 'Arabi was known in the West as Ibn Al 'Arabi and in Spain as Ibn Suraqa. However, in the east, he was generally known as Ibn Arabi without the definite 'Al' to differentiate between him and the Elder Abu Bakr of Seville who also was called Ibn Al 'Arabi. Note: Again what appears to be another coincidence. The name Abu Bakr in the traditional teachings of Islam is stated to be the first Caliph after the death of Muhammed. Today,

however, this is debated between the Shi'a and Sunni Muslims. Taught also in traditional Islam is the claim that the sermons and speeches that were made by Muhammed were written down by one of his followers, Abu Bakr. Another seeming coincidence, in Christianity it is taught that Joseph and Jesus were carpenters. Legend has it that Ali, the father of Ibn Arabi, was a carpenter and was childless for a long time. This legend goes on to say that he met the pious Muhiyuddin Abdul Qadir Jilani and requested him to pray to God to bestow on him a male child. Accordingly, the Pious Jilani who was very near the end of his life prayed for a son and told Ali to name the child Muhiyuddin after him. The legend also said that the pious Jilani blessed the prospective child in a special way and prophesied that the child would be the master of all divine secrets. Months later Muhiyuddin Ibn Al 'Arabi was born. His father Ali being in affluent circumstances gave his son, as he grew up, the best education available in his early life. Then we have what appears to be a host of antitheses.

In today's traditional teachings of Islam, Muhammed grew up as a poor orphan in very miserable circumstances. Arabi in his early tutoring developed intelligence and was quick to grasp subjects that were taught to him. Even as a student, he was head and shoulders above others. His avarice for knowledge knew no bounds that caused him forever seeking after the naked truth. As a young adult, he became famous and people came from far and near to meet him. Arabi spent his spare time with elderly men who were considered by him to be wise in their thinking. He mastered many languages, thereby, developing an immense vocabulary over the languages he spoke. At an early age in his life, he began to write fine and eloquent poetry and his prose writings became famous throughout Africa. His sharp vocabulary, sparkling intelligence and splendid memory helped him to master mystic thoughts learned from the elder mystics of his day. Ibn Al 'Arabi developed most of these aforementioned feats during his adolescent years. When grown to manhood, he began to display signs of prophetic greatness, and almost all those qualities that are essential for a <u>Prophet</u>. It also was said that he possessed a clear and unsoiled heart a supreme imagination and a strong psychic insight into dreams, telepathy, psychometry, and clairvoyance. In stark contrast, traditional Islamic teachings tell us that the Prophet Muhammed was illiterate.

Arabi was adding knowledge through sources, which were not available to the ordinary students who were seeking a higher understanding through knowledge. One source for Arabi was dreams in which he was a strong believer in them. Dreams, it is said is a very important element of Prophethood. Not only did Arabi have extraordinary dreams; he was a strong believer in them. Legend has it that Arabi would say often, "a man must endeavor to have presence of mind in dreams so that he may be the master of his thoughts, which he has gathered as a results of reasoning, even in sleep as waking. If a man gets this presence of mind and makes it to become part of his habit, he will get its fruit in the intermediate world and be highly benefited by it. Every man must strive to attain this habit, for it will be of great use." These prophetic qualities began to manifest in Arabi in his later teen years and early adult years to the point that Arabi began to tell others that he had received the emblem of discipleship from God.

Note: The term God was used in the time of Arabi (1165-1240) and not the term Allah as used in today's Islam.

It is said that Arabi use to say that he knew the great name of God and that he knew alchemy not by acquisition but through supernatural sources. Shaikh Ibn Al 'Arabi had already grown famous throughout North and Northeast Africa in places such as Egypt, Turkey, Arabia, Syria, and other areas of the African continent. He was known as a brilliant scholar, a mystic and monist of great repute and last, but not least, of all as a great occultist and spiritualist. One of the teachers of Shaikh Al 'Arabi in his early adult life was an old lady by the name of Fatima Bint Al Waliyyah. She was ninety-five years of age, but still hale and hearty and was said to have had the sight of God in everything she taught him. Note: The name Fatima in the traditional teachings of Islam today is stated to be the daughter of the traditional Prophet Muhammed. I must continue to emphasize the deliberately contrived and ascribed descriptions of a traditional Muhammed compared to the life of Arabi in order to get you to use your analytical mind and realize where these names such as Fatima, Abu Bakr, and Ali that are used in today's Islam emanated.

The following are some of the particulars that are available about the early life of Ibn Al 'Arabi. By the time he left Spain, he had earned a name as a scholar of rare eminence; his fame began to spread far and wide, which caused princes to invite him to be their secretary. He acted as secretary to a wealthy prince, but soon resigned his post, deciding to leave Spain in the year (1202) for Africa; he began to visit some of the cities of Northern Africa until he reached Egypt. He lived in Egypt for two years. During this stay, his fame immensely increased. This resulted in jealousy and opposition among his peers. This opposition even caused Arabi to be arrested, but later released. He then was forced to leave Egypt and his immense following in search of a safer and calmer atmosphere. However, let me point out that the ordinary citizen of Egypt gave him high praises because of his sayings and musings that were laced with monistic tendencies, closely interwoven with popular beliefs and mythology of a highly imaginative character. This created for him an immense following of scholars, nobles, and ordinary men. His vast knowledge and deep insight into the character and nature of human souls enabled him to be able to talk to men of all shades of opinions in their own languages. He was admired every where he went in Egypt for his marvelous character, peaceful intentions, broad toleration, his immense piety, wonderful scholarship, and deep insight into the realities of life's existence. By this time his fame had reached far and wide.

Noted scholars of his day came from distant lands to receive his blessings and learn from him truths of the upper world and the realities of the lower world. He became famous as a mystic (Sufi) of high order, a composer of elegant mystic verses and writer of immense volumes on the most abstruse and difficult subjects. His fame for innovation in style, language and method of presenting the most shocking truths clad in popular beliefs and Monophysitic mythology spread like wildfire. Not only did noted scholars seek after Arabi, but kings and princes also sought after him for his blessings and company. After leaving Egypt, he traveled to the country that was named for him after his death in later years. This country today is Saudi Arabia archaic "Araby."

Legend has it that he settled in the old Arabian city of commerce, today called Jeddah, the city next to the Red Sea, which was in the Hejaz, an Arabian region, that was under Seljukian Turkish authority during the time of the Crusades and later a part of the Ottoman Empire until 1916.

Let's continue to follow some of the activities in the life of AL 'Arabi. After living in the Hejaz area of Arabia for seven years, he then left the Hejaz and went further east in Arabia to Baghdad, an area in Iraq today. He remained there for about two or more years traveling throughout east Arabia on his white horse. After leaving Arabia, he traveled on to Syria. After staying a short time there, he left and went back to the Hejaz region in Arabia. Close by was Macoraba that was renamed Mecca. By this time, his fame had spread even more throughout the Monophysitic world. Wherever Arabi went, he performed his created ritual, called the "Pilgrimage of the Hajj." Arabi symbolically performed the Hajj in which water was poured in a circle after which Arabi began to go around and around in this circle throwing stones and chanting prayers that signified the casting out or getting rid of personal sin. Today in Mecca, the Kaaba Shrine is used to perform this ritual. It is used in the Islamic ritual of the Hajj in conjunction with chanting prayers and casting or throwing stones in the circle of supposed holy water or the spring of supposed Ishmael, called the "Zem-Zem."

Note: The definition of the term Mecca is defined as any place that one yearns to go; anything that one greatly desires or tries to achieve.

Arabi's created rituals began to be accepted and used by his many followers throughout the Monophysite world. Remember that there was no religion called Islam at the time of Arabi (1165-1240 A.D.). There was only Christianity and a Monphysite ideology that later evolved into Monist Muhammedanism beginning in 1239 and then Islam after the Koran was first formulated in Syria in 1870. Remember the Koran was finished for the very first time in history and accepted by the Muhammedan World in 1919 in Cairo, Egypt. The scattered Arab tribes throughout the Arab world were united under this one book, the Koran.

It was Arabi's stay in the Hejaz region and afterward he developed the pilgrimage of the Hajj ritual, he wrote a systematic treatise on religious matters. He used this system over a period of time to document acquired and revealed knowledge and wisdom. This system was to put his dreams, wanderings, illusions, musings, and visions in writing. Ibn Al 'Arabi put his thoughts in his first major comprehensive work, his book entitled, *Al Futuhat Al Makkiyya.* This work is also known as his Meccan Revelations.

The *Al Futuhat Al Makkiyya* is the chief work of Ibn Al 'Arabi. The author claims that every word of it was inspired by supernatural sources and it contains nothing but truths and realities. The book is now available in four large volumes that first appeared in hand written form at Bulak, Egypt in the year 1274, thirty-four years after the death of Arabi in 1240. Back then selected scholars who considered it an honor to copy Arabi's works made several copies of them as well as other writings of other old scholars whose works were available. The writings of Ibn Al 'Arabi is the least known to the modern world. Until the 1930's, no systematic study of the works of Ibn Al 'Arabi had been attempted. Even for such as R.A. Nicholson and E.G. Browne, they found it difficult and not possible to understand Arabi's writings. To understand Arabi, one has to get saturated with the mythology created by Arabi, which is being used in present day Islam, and the Koran. Getting back to *Al Futuhat Al Makkiyya*, it contains 560 chapters of which chapter 559 contains a summary of the whole and is a supposed treatise of religion and faith. The use of the word of God and his nature is discussed in several parts of the book under different headings. Note: During the time of Arabi and in his writings, the term <u>Allah</u> is absent. Some scholars argue the term Allah (the God) is a borrowed term and is an Arabized form of the Christian Syriac, Ala Ha. However, it is easier to believe that the term Allah was created for the religion called Islam. Remember the religion that is called Islam today was originally called Muhammedanism whose followers are called Moslems, meaning true believer. In the *Fusus Al Hikam (the Bezels of Wisdom)*, the supposed second book written by Arabi, you will find the absence of the name or term Allah. God also is used instead. I will discuss the *Fusus Al Hikam* as you read further. Continuing with the *Futuhat*, it is said that there are chapters dealing with the soul, its nature, origin, etceteras. The question of prophethood and inspiration has been tackled in detail. The questions regarding predestination, day of judgement, punishment and reward as well as hell and heaven have been fully discussed in the *Futuhat* by Arabi along with many more topics. Some of those are the throne of God, all principles of jurisprudence, law, and mystic or Sufi Theology.

The *Futuhat Al Makkiyya* was written in the most abstruse or hard to understand manner so that it might not be possible for the credulous theologians or the common man to understand it. As previously mentioned, after *Al Futuhat* came the second book, *Fusus Al Hikam, The Bezels of Wisdom or Mosaic of Precepts.* This book was undertaken in Damascus, Syria in the beginning of 1227 A.C.E. and completed near the end of 1230 A.C.E.

I will discuss this book as a main topic as you read further. I will continue to follow the life and biography of Ibn Al 'Arabi as he moves from place to place in Africa. While in Africa, Ibn Al 'Arabi not only wrote his two best known works, he also wrote and kept a diary of his sayings (thoughts of his spiritual revelations) or his "Hadith," a term used today in Islamic tradition among the Moslems for the sayings of Muhammed.

I will continue to use the translation of Moulavi S.A.Q. Husaini M.A. to give an example of the "Sayings" of Ibn Al 'Arabi.

Sayings of Ibn Al 'Arabi or Hadith

1. The speech of a knower must be in accordance with

the understanding of the hearer, his weakness and permanent hidden prejudices.

2. If you find it difficult to answer anyone, do not answer him. His vessel is full and he does not require an answer.

3. An ass knows more than one who knows only something about the unity of God.

4. Flee from suspicion.

5. Many people give direct opposite interpretations to sayings of scholars.

6. If a knower gives out what passes in his mind, the veterans consider him to be ignorant; the orthodox retorts and shuns him. The truth is, God has given His beloved, miracles which are but a kind of the miracles of Prophets. It is not improper to talk in their own way because some scholars are not able to understand them.

7. If one does not believe in what a group says, he must not keep their company; for company without understanding is a fatal poison.

8. Close proximity is a veil just like great distance is one. If God is nearer to us than the jugular vein, where are the seventy thousand veils?

9. Do not admit doubt in knowledge of Divine secrets, for its proper place is in the exact sciences.

10. The qualification of a perfect man is his generosity towards his enemies who do not know the nature and character of God and call themselves his enemies on account of their ignorance although he (the perfect man) is always generous towards them.

11. The qualification of a Shaikh is that he should possess all that the Mur īd (disciple) may require of him, not miracles and illumination.

12. The Sufi is one who drops away the three "I's." He shall not say li (for me), nor 'indi (with me) not mat ā'i (my wealth). That is, he must not attribute anything to himself.

13. Supplication is the marrow of worship. It is through the marrow that the limbs are strong. Similarly, it is by supplication that the devotion of a worshiper is strengthened.

14. A man cannot attain the stage of perfect knowledge, if he ignores a single injunction of any of the prophets' religions. He who claims this stage and transgresses any of the injunctions of the faith or any other faith is a liar.

15. Complete ignorance of God is sure knowledge of God.

16. The names of God on which the existence of the universe is based are but four, the Living, the Mighty, the Seeker and the Knower, and it is through these four names that His being a God is proved.

17. He, who deviates from the Code, never attains anything, though his fame may reach the heavens.

18. God, the merciful, has prohibited the blind following of Malik, Ahmed, No'man or others.

19. I am not a man who says Ibn Hazam said so and so, Ahmed said so and so and No'man said so and so.

20. O Pearl Divine, white Pearl that is in a shell of dark mortality art made to dwell! alas, while common gems we prize and hoard, thy worth inestimable is still ignored!

Throughout the life of Ibn Al 'Arabi, there were people who enjoyed intercourse with him, thereby, having a personal Sahaba (or contact) with him in which some spoke highly of him while others denounced him.

The following are some of the dialogue from these encounters. One group led by Ibn Al Taimia Al Taftazani and Ibrahim Al Biqa'I denounced him as an infidel and charged him with the advocacy of practicing <u>Monism</u>. While another group headed by Majduddin, Suyuti who considered him to be a great saint, prophet, Siddiq (k), and Sufi of a high order. Unfortunately, the exact remarks of Shaikh Ibn Al 'Arabi's opponents and the charges leveled against him can only be found in the writings of his defenders. Another follower of Arabi was Allamah Jamaluddin who writes of him "I saw Muhiyuddin at Damascus. He was the greatest of the scholars of his time. He combined in him all the qualities that are conferred by God. He had scholars and ordinary people falling in line to follow him." Time has revealed the opinions of scholars and others who wrote about Arabi. Their writings have varied from infidelity to saintship. Some called him a Zindiq (k) or heretic and others called him a Siddiq (k) or he who always accepts or confirms the truth. While some went to the lowest extreme and called him an apostle of Satan. Another interesting story concerning Ibn Al 'Arabi was the one written by Shaikh 'Izzuddin Ibn 'Abd Al Salam who relates to the time in his classroom when a student asked him the question as to who he thought was the most eminent saint of our age? He answered and said Shaikh Muhiyuddin Ibn Al 'Arabi. In the following pages I will give a short overview on some of Ibn Al 'Arabi's views on certain important topics such as god, prophethood, saintship, and Messengership. Again, this is done with the translation of Moulavi S.A.Q. Husaini who translated Arabi's works into English.

Ibn Al 'Arabi on God

God is and nothing is with him. This is translated also to mean that existence is identical with him (God) for it is manifested through it. (Al Futuhat Al Makkiyya, Vol. 2, page 56.) (2) "God by himself makes man obey when he is so pleased and also judges in accordance with the injunctions given to him. It is obligation that has given rise to the term the "worshipped." "There is no might or strength except through God." God leads you to good actions and rewards you. So is he designated the "Magnanimous." If heaven be the reward for what you have done, where is the magnanimity is of God, which attributed to him? You are bestowed the knowledge that you are for yourself. But you are not given the knowledge that you are for yourself. But you are for the knowledge about the origin of yourself. If you are not the author of what you seek recompense for, how do you view your actions? Cast off the things and their Creator, the sustained and the sustainer. (Al Futuhat Al Makkiyya, Vol. I, page 2.) (3) God is the spirit and the form of the universe. We must not say that the universe is but form of which he is the spirit. (Fusus Al Hikam, page 132 and 146). (4) All things are attributes of God; as such they are ultimately identical with God apart from whom they are nothing. (Fusus Al Hikam, pages 132 and 146.) (5) The whole infinite series of individualizations are in fact one eternal and everlasting manifestation, which never repeats itself. (Fusus Al Hikam, pages 153 and 239.)

Ibn Al 'Arabi on Prophethood

Know that prophethood of man is two kinds. The first kind is from God to man without an angelic spirit between him and God. This office gives him divine information, which he finds in his own self from the hidden source or through revelations. This information does not include allowance or prohibition, but only impart divine knowledge or knowledge about the truth of the code rules.

The second kind of human prophethood is of men who can be called the disciples of angels. The trustworthy spirit comes with a code, in their opinion from God. He allows whatever he likes and forbids whatever he dislikes. These things took place before the days of my being. Today, there is no value to such revelations. It is the function of the angels. (*Al Futuhat Al Makkiyya*, Vol. 2, pages 254-55) (1) Prophethood will continue till the day of resurrection in the world. Providing a code is but one function of prophethood. It is impossible that the information from God and the knowledge of his universe should discontinue. If it discontinues, it will not be possible for the universe to get food for its existence and continuance. "Say, if the ocean were ink for the words of God exhausted, should we seek help from things of its kind. If all the trees were to be pens and all the oceans were to be ink. God has informed that there is not a single thing which was created without the word "Be." These words of God never discontinue. They are the sustenance for the universe and all existence. If providing a code, which is but one aspect of prophethood ends. Where are the other aspects? *(Al Futuhat*, Vol. 2, page 90).

Ibn Al 'Arabi on Saintship

There are four grades of goodness bestowed on man. They are:

1. Iman (belief)
2. Wilayat (Saintship)
3. Nubuwat (Prophethood)
4. Risalat (Messengership)

Knowledge is essential for saintship, which is friendship with God; and it is not necessary for belief. For belief depends on information and does not require knowledge as to the whereabouts of God or his possibility and so on. Saints are the first-class scholars of oneness; for God never takes an ignorant person as his friend. This is a big question, which the customary scholars have overlooked. A solution of this question will include all Monotheists under one sky, whatever may be the path pursued by them. (Al Futuhat, Vol. 2, Page 52)

Ibn Al 'Arabi on Messengership

Verily Messengership is bestowed. The recipient of this bounty need not desire it. He is born just, wise, knowing, and comprehending. Neither knowledge nor action nor holiness is condition precedent to it; but custom sees a prophet inclined towards good and pleasant moods.

(Al Futuhat, Vol. 2, page 256).   Messengership is an intermediary state between the sender and the sent. It is not an absolute situation but only a relative one and ceases to exist the moment the message is delivered. God says: "The messenger has but to deliver."   This is incumbent on him.   He further says: "O messenger, deliver what is sent unto you from your lord." If you do not do it, you have not delivered his message. (Al Futuhat, Vol. 2, pages 258-259).

In the year preceding the death of IBN Al" Arabi (1239) his disciples who were his faithful followers and biographers, began to use his religious practices as a guide for their new Monist religion. They then began to use his life, character, sayings, writings, and customs to venerate the Shaikh Al' Akbar Muhiyuddin IBN Al' Ali, a.k.a., Ibn Al' Arabi Alias Muhammed. Whereby, the meaning of his name "Muhammed" became to mean "one who is worthy of praise."   This caused a new orthodox system of rites or (Tarika) rituals, laws, and customs for his disciples and followers to use as their foundation for their new monist religion that they called Muhammedanism.   Again, the religion called "Islam" today was originally called "Muhammedanism."   It is based on a Monist ideology, a doctrine that says, "there is only one ultimate substance or principal."

Note: Today in traditional Islamic teachings, this ideology is worded to say that there is but one God and Allah is his name. This Monist ideology was used by Arabi and taught to his followers who began to spread his teachings.

Muhammedanism began to spread with the strong help of the Ottoman Turks in the late 13th and early 14[th centuries], who began to enforce this new Monist religion throughout North Africa, i.e., Egypt, Libya, Tunisia, Algeria, Morocco, and Mauritania. It also began to spread across the Mediterranean Sea into Spain, into the southern areas of Europe, the Balkans, the home of the Bogomils (today Serbs), Bulgaria, Yugoslavia, Albania, Greece, parts of China, Indonesia, and Asiatic Russia.

The countries of Northeast Africa, i.e., Turkey, and other land regions that are known today as Iran, Iraq, Syria, Jordan, Palestine, Lebanon, Saudi Arabia, Kuwait, and Yemen were all part of the Ottoman Empire at one time. However, today these land areas in North and Northeast Africa are grouped under one umbrella and renamed the "Middle East" by Europeans. The purpose of the Europeans doing this was to create this part of the world as the "Land of the Bible." Why? Because it puts all three man-made religions, Christianity, Islam, and Judaism in close proximity to something that is real, Ancient Egypt. In contrast man-made religions are based on Mythology, e.g., Christianity, Islam, and Judaism, etc. Ancient Egypt is something that existed pre-biblically along with its many monuments and immortal legacies, the Great Pyramid and the Sphinx have continued. Ancient Egypt still exists outside of religion and religious literature. On the other hand, Christianity and Islam need the Bible and the Koran respectively, and Judaism needs the Sefer Ha Torah, which is the writings of Maimoinedes' Pentateuch, and other pirki avot apocryphal writings to sustain them. Ancient Egypt does not need literature to make it real or literature to sustain it, or believers to give it life whereas all man-created religions and all religious literature need believers to give them life.

Note: A major effort has been underway for over fifty years since the creation of Israel to create Bibleland, and thus legitimize the three major religions.

The Ottoman Turks began to approach their conquered subjects or brethren at the beginning of the 14th century with a forceful outcry of "Muhammed or die." With the on slaught of Muhammedanism in Africa, Spain, and Europe this new Monist religion began to spread into other areas of the world, such as India (Pakistan), Afghanistan, and the Mongolian area in Europe. This caused the animistic and monophysitic thinking of the local indigenous African Berbers and Bedouins to lose their old traditions, customs, and culture. Similarly, the European Arabs living in the same land areas, including the Balkans and Asiatic Russia had their monophysitic thinking replaced with Orthodox Monist Muhammedanism that was later updated to Islam when the Koran was created. Arabi's devotion and practice of religious piety have been renamed in today's traditional Islam as Sufism. Another less familiar name for Sufism is Tasawwuf, also known as Theosophy. It is safe to say that Ibn Arabi was the world's first Sufi given that he laid the foundation for the monist religion we know now as Muhammedanism/Islam and Sufism today is associated with Islam. During the first three centuries following the enforcement of Muhammedanism by the Ottoman Turks, the Sufi movement also developed.

The original disciples and followers of Arabi in this movement were mostly men of the local regions. They were often illiterate and their aim was to attract and convert their fellow countrymen to the mystical principles of monist Muhammedanism and Eastern Sufism, which was created by its founder, Ibn Al' Arabi. The followers of Arabi began to worship him as the Muhammed, "one who is worthy of praise." Al Sheik Al' Akbar Muhiyuddin Ibn Al' Arabi was adapted and adopted as "Muhammed the Prophet," their god, whom they worshipped prior to switching to the God Rahman, "The Compassionate," whose name was used preceding every Sura. In the early Orthodox version of the Koran, Rahman was in use instead of Allah. Similarly, centuries prior the Melchite Coptic Egyptians took the image of the Greek Ruler Ptolemy I Lagi and created his image into Serapis and gave him the attributes of Osiris and Apis, the sacred bull. Subsequently, the image of Serapis through a series of Council meetings later became Christ, the god of Christianity. See *The Historical Origin of Christianity.*

Legend has it that after his death Arabi left his "Badal" or double behind in the form of the created traditional prophet of Islam "Muhammed." Another way to assist in one's understanding in the creation of Muhammed is to know that in Christianity as aforementioned, Serapis became the "Christ" and in Muhammedanism/Islam, the biography and life of Ibn Al

Arabi became the Prophet "Muhammed." The life and character of Ibn Al' Arabi as portrayed by his earliest biographers, who were faithful followers and disciples, leave no doubt that he was thoroughly human and liable to error. Today, however, Islamic traditional teachings have changed all this. Muhammed now is sinless and almost divine. The two hundred and one titles of honor given to Muhammed proclaim his godliness. Through the process of time the Muhammedan/Islamic world gave to Muhammed some of the attributes of Christ and for all practical purposes Muhammed is the Moslem Christ. I will now quote Carter G. Woodson, the author of The Mis-Education of the Negro, "If you can control a man's thinking, you do not have to worry about his actions." These words are as true today as they were when written in 1933. So, I urge you not to allow any man-made religion to control your thinking. Further, I urge you to do as I have done, and that was to research, research, research, and research until you find the most logical facts concerning the subject at hand.

CHAPTER VII
THE DECLINE OF MUHAMMEDANISM
AND THE RISE OF ISLAM

With the onslaught of the Seljuk Turks against the Byzantine Empire beginning in 1079, the stage was set for the Crusades in Africa in 1096, which eventually led to the loss of most of their empire. The empire was later reduced to the limits of its capital, the city of Constantinople.

In 1293 a Mongolian Turkish tribal chieftain, Othman or Osman I, overran his brethren the Seljuk Turks and founded an empire in Western Asia Minor (Turkey). His empire was to endure for a little over six centuries (1300-1919). As this empire grew by conquering lands throughout the Byzantine Empire and beyond. They began to enforce and spread Muhammedanism, a monist religion that became the foundation of Islam. Muhammedanism is based on the biography and actual life of Ibn Al 'Arabi, the African from Spain, which was started by his disciples and followers sixty-one years earlier (1239) a religion that was still in its developing orthodox stages. With the sword and the cry "Muhammed or Die," this religious ideology began to spread all over the Ottoman Empire as mentioned in Chapter VI. During this time in history, Christianity was practiced only in certain areas of Europe, i.e., Rome, Italy, France, Germany) and not in the areas of the Ottoman African Empire as aforementioned with one exception, the Church of Hagia Sophia in the city of Constantinople. The Hagia Sophia fell in 1453 to the Ottoman Turks under the Sultan Muhammed II.

I will walk you through Ottoman Turkish history as it developed over the centuries of its existence starting with the early empire, 1300-1441. The Dynasty that Osman I founded (1258-1326) was called Osmanli, meaning "Sons of Osman." The name evolved from English into Ottoman. The Empire expanded under Osman I and his successors, Orkhan (ruled 1326-1359) and Murad I (ruled 1359-1389) especially in Western Asia Minor and Southeastern Europe, and the Balkan Peninsula primarily. During Orkhan's reign, he began the practice of recruiting boys and young men to become soldiers and administrators. As soldiers, they filled the ranks of the infantry and were known as the Janizaries (also spelled Janissaries), who developed into the most fearsome military force in Africa and Europe for centuries.

Next came Murad I, during his reign he used the Janizaries to conquer Thrace the area Northwest of Constantinople in 1361. He then moved his capital to Adrianople, which was the second largest city of the Byzantine Empire. This conquest effectively cut off Constantinople from the outside world. With Adrianople being the capital, this controlled the principal invasion route through the Balkan Mountains, giving the Ottomans access to further expansion to the North in Europe. During the last victorious battle of Murad I against Balkan enemies, he was killed. His successor was Bayezid I (1389-1402).

Bayezid I was unable to penetrate further north into Europe. Instead, he was forced to devote his attention to the eastern area of Turkey to deal with the uprising of the Turkish strong man, Karaman. He attacked and defeated Karaman in 1391, and then went on to put down a revolt of his Balkan subjects, and returned to consolidate his gains in victory. His successes attracted the attention of Timur Lenk (Tamerlane) who was encouraged by Turkish Princes who had fled to Tamerlane's court from Bayezid I's incursions. Tamerlane attacked and overwhelmed Bayezid in 1402. Taken captive by Timur Lenk, Bayezid died within a year.

Timur Lenk held on to this empire from 1402 to 1413 and then retired from Asia Minor, leaving Bayezid's sons to take up where their father had failed. The four sons fought for control until one of them Muhammed I, killed the other three and took control. He reigned from 1413 to 1421. Murad II succeeded him.

Murad II reigned from 1421 to 1451. He suppressed Balkan resistance that threatened his sovereignty in the area. The task of finishing the Balkan conquests and seizing all of Asia Minor fell to Murad II's successor, the Sultan Muhammed II who ruled from 1451-1481. It was he who completed the siege of Constantinople in 1453 and made it the capital of the Ottoman Empire. With the conquest of the Queen of all cities to his credit, Muhammed II incorporated the Crimea in Russia on the north coast of the Black Sea. Note: More will be said about Muhammed II in Chapter IX. And, remember that all Ottoman rulers continued to spread and enforce Monist "Muhammedanism" throughout the Empire and not Islam, as today's modern history books would have you to believe.

Islam was non-existent until the formulation and completion of the Koran that was accepted by the Muhammedan world in 1919 in Cairo, Egypt. In addition to conquering a large empire that included the Byzantine City of Constantinople and the first seat (See) of Christianity, Church of Hagia Sophia; Muhammed II worked strenuously to consolidate his empire to its greatest height. Following Muhammed II to the throne of Ottoman power was his sons Bayezid II (1481-1512), his grandson Selim I (1512-1520), and his Great grandson, Suleyman I, The Magnificent (1520-66). Bayezid extended the Empire in Europe, added outposts along the Black Sea, and put down revolts in Asia Minor. He also turned the Ottoman fleet into a major Mediterranean naval power. Later in his life, he became feeble in his thinking and was replaced on the throne by his more militant son, Selim I, who took the task to eliminate all competition for his position. He had his brothers, their sons, and all but one of his own sons killed. He then established control over the army, which wanted to select its own candidate to power. An added benefit of efforts by Selim I was the control of all Northeast African trade routes between Africa and Europe. The growth of the empire had for some time been an impediment to European trade. At this time, this led European states to seek routes around Africa to China and India. It also impelled the Europeans to travel westward, which led them to the discovery of other areas in the Americas. It was Selim's surviving son, Suleyman who came to the throne in an enviable situation. New revenues from the expanded empire left him with wealth and power unparalleled in Ottoman history. In his early campaigns, he captured Belgrade (1521) and Rhodes (1522) and broke the military power of Hungary. In 1529 He laid siege to Vienna, Austria, but was forced to withdraw for lack of supplies.

In Constantinople, Suleyman built The Magnificent Mosque, Suleymaniye Cami, which was named for him. During his 46-year reign, the Ottoman Empire was at the height of its political power and close to its maximum geographical extent. The seeds of decline, however, were already planted. As Suleyman grew tired of campaigns and retired to his harem, his Viziers, or Prime ministers, took more authority. After his death, the army gained the Sultanate and was able to use it for its own benefit. Few Sultans after Suleyman had the ability to exercise real power when the need arose. This weakness at home was countered by a growing power in the west. The nation-states of Europe were emerging from the Middle Ages under strong monarchies. They were building armies and navies that were combined fleets from Venice, Spain, and the Papal State of Italy. They defeated the Turks in the Great Naval Battle of Lepanto off the coast of Greece. This defeat, which dispelled the myth of the invincible Turk, took place during the reign of Selim II (1566-1574). However, the Empire was able to rebuild its navy and continued to control the eastern Mediterranean for another century.

As the central government became weaker, large parts of the empire began to act independently, retaining only nominal loyalty to the Sultan. This weakness played well in the hands of their enemies. Also during this time the Monist Muhammedan religion that was in use throughout the Ottoman Empire began to take on a new direction. This was due to the many sects that had developed over the centuries without any organized guidelines to follow. They had only a few Arabi rituals, but no laws or religious literature to guide them. However, during this period in history religious literature, such as the Old and New Testaments for the Christians had been printed and in use. The Muhammedans, however, had no written or printed literature. The Koran had not been created or formulated. The cohesiveness of Muhammedanism began to decline. However, the army was still strong enough to prevent provincial rebels from asserting complete control.

Under Murad III (ruled 1574-1595) new campaigns were undertaken. The Caucasus was conquered, and Azerbaijan was seized. This brought the empire to the peak of its territorial extent. Twenty-nine years later the Ottomans were driven out of the Caucasus and Azerbaijan (1603). However, under the rule of Murad IV (ruled 1623-40), the Empire remained strong in the east. Five years after the reign of Murad IV a war with Venice (1645-1669) exposed Constantinople to an attack by the Venetian Navy. In 1683 the last attempt to conquer Vienna failed. At this time Russia and Austria began to attack the empire by direct military contact and by causing revolts by non-Muhammedan subjects of the Sultan.

In 1683, with the failed attack on Vienna, the Ottomans were at war with other European enemies for 41 years. As a result, the empire lost much of its Balkan territory and all of the possessions on the shores of the Black Sea. From this time foreword, the Ottoman Sultans were beginning to loose control. The Austrians and Russians were allowed to intervene in the affairs of the Empire. The weakness of the central government was manifested by its military decline that showed itself in a gradual loss of control over most of the provinces. Local rulers, called notables, carved for themselves permanent regions in which they ruled directly, regardless of the wishes of the Sultan in Constantinople. The notables were able to build their power bases because local populations preferred their rule to the corrupt administration of the faraway capital in Constantinople. The notables formed their own armies and collected their own taxes, sending only nominal contributions to the imperial treasury.

When Selim III (ruled 1789-1807) came to the throne, he attempted to reform the empire and its army. He failed and was overthrown. After Selim III came Mahmud II (ruled 1808-1839) to the throne, the empire was in desperate straits. Control of North Africa had passed to local notables. In Egypt, for instance, Muhammed Ali (1806) was laying the foundation for an independent kingdom. At this point, had the European nations cooperated with each other, they could have destroyed the

Ottoman Empire. At the same time more notables or local rulers began to spring up all over Africa and beyond, which further caused the Ottoman Sultans to loose internal control of their empire.

Let's proceed further in Ottoman history. In 1826, five years after Greece began to fight for independence, the Janizares, the Royal Army, of the empire revolted to stop reforms. Mahmud II had them massacred and constructed a new military system in the style of European armies. He also reformed the administration and gained control over some of the provincial notables, with the exception of the notables in Egypt. By the time of Mahmud's death the empire was strong in some areas and weak in other areas. However, it was still subject to European interference. Mahmud's sons, Abulmedici I (ruled 1839-1861) and Abulaziz (ruled 1861-1876) carried out further reforms, especially in education and law.

It was during the reign of Abulaziz that the creation, formulation and writing of the Koran first came into existence. The first creation and formulation started in 1870 in the region of Syria by Jewish scholars and Rabbis. This group of scholars came from the Alliance Israelite Universelle of Paris, France who sent them there for that purpose. After 49 years of development with the help of Christian and Arab Scholars using Christian (Four Gospels) and Jewish (Pentateuch and Psalms), the Koran was finally finished and accepted by the Muhammedan world in 1919 in Cairo, Egypt. With this book, The Koran, it gave birth to a new religious ideology called "Islam." Thus, the scattered Muhammedan world that was controlled by the notables in Africa began to unify themselves around this book. The focus was no longer on Muhammed as God or the Divine of God, but the focus was now on the new God of the Koran which was the God-Rahman who was later replaced by Allah who became the One God of Islam. The Muhammedans, however, had called themselves Moslems to identify themselves as followers of Ibn Al Arabi, alias Muhammed and now Islam. More will be said about the Koran as you read further in this chapter. Let's get back to the declining years of the Ottoman Empire.

By the middle of the nineteenth century, it was evident that the Ottoman cause was hopeless. Czar Nicholas I of Russia commented on the Ottoman Empire in 1853: "We have on our hands a sick man, a very sick man." However, conflict between the European states kept the Ottoman Empire in power until after World War I. This is especially true of Great Britain, who was determined to keep Russia from gaining direct access to the Mediterranean from the Black Sea. This effort by Britain, France and others, however, did not stop Russia in the Russo-Turkish War of 1877-1878 when Constantinople almost was captured. If the Russians had defeated the Turks, most likely the Ottomans would have been forced to sign the harsh treaty of "San Steffano." This would have ended their rule in Europe except for the European states that made up the Congress of Berlin. This Congress succeeded in propping up the old Empire for a few more decades.

Note: The British and the French did not want Russia to topple the Ottoman Empire. This was because of the vast oil reserves under Turkish control in such areas as Arabia, today Iraq and today Kuwait. The British did, however, topple the Ottoman Empire during World War I (1914-1918).

Abudulhamid (ruled 1876-1909) developed strong ties with Germany, and the Ottomans fought on Germany's side in World War I. Russia hoped to use the war as an excuse to gain access to the Mediterranean and, perhaps, capture Constantinople. This aim was frustrated by the Russian Revolution of 1917, which caused the Russians to withdraw from the war. The Ottoman defeat in World War I inspired an already fervent Turkish nationalism among the Turks. Muhammed VI fled in 1922 after the Sultanate had been abolished. All members of the Ottoman Dynasty were expelled from the country two years later. But the post war settlement of land areas that was controlled and issued out by the British outraged the Nationalists. A new government in Turkey was established with the help of the British under the leadership of Mustafa Kemal, known as Ataturk, who emerged in 1923 at Ankara and began to westernize Turkey in an attempt to stamp out all traces of the culture and ways of the Ottoman Turks. The British with the help of its allies had destroyed the Ottoman Empire during World War I. As a reminder, I reiterate that the British took control of key land areas in Northeast Africa; today renamed the "Middle East." This new name was part of a plan designed to keep the world from thinking of this land area as being part of the African continent. "Middle

East," became a political name designed by the Zionists that made this area the land of the Old and the New Testament Bibles for the convenience of the Zionist Jews. The British executed this caper after they promised the Jews a section of Palestine to create an illegal and political homeland, to be called Israel. A deal was made between the British, Arthur James Balfour, hence, the Balfour Declaration of 1917, Lord Lionel Walter Rothschild, of the Zionist Federation in England, and the Zionist Chaim Weizman who became the first President of Israel in 1948.

With the name "Middle East" the Zionists with assistance from the British Imperialists were able to set in place pseudo monuments in Jerusalem that would represent the three major religions. The "Wailing Wall For Jews, for example, the "Church of the Holy Sepulcher" for the Christians, the "Dome of the Rock Mosque" for the Moslems, and to further develop the city of Jerusalem for this purpose. See Chapter IX for more details about Jerusalem.

The name Middle East also was supposed to keep the populace of the world from knowing and realizing that the illegal state of Israel is in Africa. Thereby, keeping the African people throughout the world from causing an outcry against the illegal political state of Israel and the uncivilized savage treatment of its neighbors. The British went on to create the country that we know today as Jordan. This was done beginning in 1916 when the British backed Sherif Hussein Ibn Ali of Arabia and his son, Faisal I, organized an Arab army to fight with other allies against the Ottoman Turks during World War I (1914-1918). The British agent T.E. Lawrence, a.k.a., Lawrence of Arabia was sent to assist. After the defeat of the Ottoman Empire, the League of Nations placed the entire region today called the Middle East in the hands of the British with the exception of Syria, which was given to France by the League of Nations in 1920. The French divided Syria and created a new state today called Lebanon. Included in the British Mandate was Palestine and what is now the East Bank of Jordan. In 1921 the British declared the region east of the River Jordan an Emirate. They put Abdullah, another son of Sherif Hussein, on the throne as Emir. Britain named the territory Transjordan. The British high commissioner of Palestine supervised Abdullah's rule.

Britain continued to give Transjordan financial aid and supported a Transjordan army made up mostly of villagers and Bedouins. Prior to this, in 1917, Britain issued The Balfour Declaration. In this Declaration, Britain promised to help establish a Jewish Zionist homeland in Palestine without violating the civil and religious rights of Palestine's non-Jewish population. But Britain also promised a homeland in Palestine to the Palestinians as well. After World War I, the British helped many Jews to settle in Palestine. This was not the first time that Jews were settled in Palestine. It started in a big way with the help of the French Baron Edmond James De Rothschild of the Rothschild banking empire in the late 1800's. When he began to purchase land and develop Jewish settlements in Palestine, he began by building 29 or more Jewish settlements. This was his way of responding to the threats facing the Jews in Europe in the late 19th century and also in response to the Socialist Zionist movement of Nathan Birnbaum, the father of Zionism.

The Arab Palestinians opposed the growing numbers of Jewish settlers. They saw Palestine as their land and considered the Jews intruders. Jewish immigration increased during the 1930's and 1940's because of the German persecution of Jews in Europe before and during World War II. Ironically, wealthy Jews and non-Jews financed this persecution under the banner of capitalism.

In 1928 Britain recognized Transjordan as an independent state and began to transform and build this region and territory into a country that is known today as Jordan.

Note: Prior to 1928, the country known, as Jordan was only a land region and territory and not a country as it is today. However, the British kept control of the country's defense, finances, and foreign affairs. Transjordan gained complete independence in 1946, or did it?

Palestinians and Zionist/Jews who are both Europeans and who are both invaders in this region of the world are occupying, claiming, and fighting over land that does not belong to them. The reason being is that this land is part of the African Continent. Therefore, it belongs to the indigenous Africans. For years, Arab Palestinians have fought Jews and the British for control of this land. In 1947, Britain who had been terrorized by the violent Zionist Stern gang in (1940-1949) was forced to ask the United Nations to help settle the conflict. The UN suggested a plan to divide Palestine into two states; one Jewish and one Arab, leaving Jerusalem under international control. The Arabs turned down the plan, but the Jews accepted it. In 1948, the British Mandate in Palestine ended and the Zionist/Jews established the illegal political state of Israel on the land assigned to them under the UN agreement. Fighting broke out between the Palestinians who were supported by several Arab States and the United States and Britain supported the Israelis. When the fighting ended in January 1949, Israel had increased its size by about half, which included a part of Jerusalem. Transjordan held the West Bank and the rest of Jerusalem. Egypt controlled an area called the Gaza Strip. Israel and Transjordan made the territory they held part of their countries. In 1950, Transjordan changed its name to Jordan. As I write this book in 2002, fighting is still taking place in this area of the African Continent, which is a misnomer and called the "Middle East."

Getting back to the subject of Islam, I will now explain things that are important to know about Islam and the Koran:

(A) Islam started from the beginning as a religion based upon a book known as the Koran. From this book, God (Allah) through his Prophet (Muhammed) passes on from God what men need to know for their own good which has been recited to him by his Angel (Gabriel) to what he called Koran, i.e., "Recital Recitation." This is suppose to account for the fact that in the Koran in contrast to the Bible, the speaker everywhere is God (Allah). Today, the Moslems always quote the Book as the word of Allah (The God), which is the general word for God in Islam, Al (The) Lah (God). These two words over the period of time got merged into one "Allah" meaning "The God."

(B) In the early orthodox version of the Koran that was created between 1870 and 1919, the name Rahman, "The Compassionate," was in use instead of Allah. Rahman occurred in the introduction preceding every Sura. Later Moslems over the period of time changed the name Rahman to Allah. The new writers of the Koran also changed the formula to read in the name of Allah, The Compassionate and Merciful," i.e., Rahman, the God, Allah, the God equals the same.

(C) Question: What happened to the Orthodox God of Islam, Rahman, "The Compassionate?" The name Rahman was used to create one of the most sacred ritual/customs in the religious practice of Islam, and that is "Ramadan" which is the name of the ninth month of the Muhammedan calendar.

(D) Ramadan is an Islamic ritual/custom copied from the Jewish tradition of Ashura, "The Day of Atonement." I will now quote excerpts from the Shorter Encyclopedia of Islam concerning Ramadan: 1. "Ramadan is the only month of the year to be mentioned in the Kur'an (Sura ii 185): "The month of Ramadan (is that) in which The Kur'an was sent down in connection with the establishment of the fast of Ramadan. The discussion on the origin of this edict cannot yet be considered ended:

"In connection with the above mentioned verse of the Kur'an calls attention to the parallelism between the mission of Muhammed and the handling of the second tablets of the law to Moses, which according to Jewish tradition took place on the day of Atonement (Ashura, the predecessor of Ramadan!) and actually was the cause of its institution."

(E) A large number of Jewish teachings, sayings, narratives, and ethical precepts have been included in the Koran. The Isnad, the Hadith, and the "Sunna," comprise the writings in which Jewish writers created the character called the Prophet Muhammed that was done under the term "Isra'iliy at" or "Isra'lite tales." Comment: What you have just read further substantiates the fact that the Prophet Muhammed of Islamic tradition is a created mythical character.

(F) Monist Muhammedanism and the Koran ended the religious argument between the Dyophysitic Christians and the Monophysites, who argued over the icon of Christ having a human nature for 921 years. Today this argument is unheard of between the Christian world and the Islamic world.

(G) With the creation and the formulation of the Koran (1870-1919) and Islam, it brought together the three major religions, Christianity, Judaism, and Islam in one book.

Let me reiterate. The Koran is an adaptation of the Jewish Sefer Ha Torah or Old Testament and the Christian Four Gospels.

Comment: The Arabs did not have enough wherewithal to create their own rituals/customs and write their own religious literature and tell their own stories. They allowed Jewish scholars and Rabbis and Christian scholars to write and produce religious literature for them, i.e., the "Koran." These scholars, thereby, created a new religion for the Arab world, "Islam."

Note: The Jews and Christians had their religious literature in print hundreds of years before the first Koran was ever produced.

I will reiterate once more that "Islam is a religion based upon a book called the Koran. Without the Koran, there is no Islam. I urge you to read this statement over and over and over again until you can internalize and understand this fact.

CHAPTER VIII
THINGS TO THINK ABOUT CONCERNING ISLAM OUTSIDE OF ISLAMIC TRADITION

There are parallels and similarities between the life of Ibn Al 'Arabi and the traditional object of Islam Muhammed. On the other hand, there are glaring dichotomies between the real life of Arabi and the traditional fictional life of Muhammed. There are no life sketches or depictions of Ibn Al 'Arabi, for example, and likewise, there are no depictions or icons of the Prophet Muhammed of traditional Islam. Of course, one of the reasons is that in Orthodox Islam, it is against religious law to do so. You may sometimes see a faceless image of a man depicted as Muhammed (See front cover of this book). This should help us to understand that the Prophet Muhammed of tradition is a man-made creature, not human. In contrast, we know,

- Arabi was born in Murcia, Spain in560 A.H. and tradition says that the Prophet Muhammed was born in Mecca in 570 A.D.
- Ibn Al 'Arabi's father was named Ali.
- Islamic traditional legends say that Ali was the cousin and the son-in-law of Muhammed, the Prophet of Islam.
- Arabi was tutored by an old lady named Fatima Bini Al-Waliyyah who was reported to be ninety-five years old.

- Islamic tradition says that the daughter of the Prophet Muhammed was named Fatima.
- Ibn Al 'Arabi was a monist, practicing a monist ideology which is a doctrine that say's "There is only one ultimate substance or principle, whether mind, (idealism) matter (materialism) or some third thing that is based on both."
- Islam teaches that there is only one god Allah (the God), which is based on Monism.
- The formulators of the Koran, which is a book, and Islam, which is a religion, were created by Jewish and Christian scholars and were approved and accepted by Muhammedan Arab scholars. The Koran was first formulated in 1870 in Syria. It was finished and accepted by the Arab Moslem world in 1919 in Cairo, Egypt. With the completion and acceptance of the Koran this caused the scattered Bedouins and other Muhammedan Tribes to unify around this book thus causing unification among themselves for the first time in their history.
- The Koran is a book that also consists of three kinds of literature, the Jewish Pentateuch and Psalms, the Christian Four Gospels, and interspersed with some Monist Muhammedan ideology that contains the doctrines of Ibn Al 'Arabi on mysticism and monism. The Jewish and Christian writings in the Koran maintain complete influence in all Muslim countries

today.

- Jewish scholars who helped create Islam and Islamic literature added to the mythology of Islam that "Safiya" was the eleventh wife of Muhammed and came from a Jewish tribe. This further proves that Jewish influence is in the fabric and construction of Islam. This also is done to get one to believe that Judaism is a B.C. religion that came before its founder Solomon bar Isaac called RASHI (1040-1105).

- With the Koran came a new name change, from Muhammedanism, to "Islam" thus the birth of a new religion.
- Geographical Mecca was called <u>Macoraba</u> before it was named Mecca. Likewise, geographical Medina was called <u>Lathrib</u> before it was named Medina. These names were in use during and after the supposed birth and death of the created Muhammed of tradition.
- Mecca and Medina are part of a systematic effort to make the Koran literal and historical. Remember Mecca and the Hajj/Pilgrimage were a mental state of mind prior to the first meeting in Islam's history that was called by Abdul Aziz in Arabia (Hejaz) in Mecca. The year was 1926.

  Note: Mecca is dated by Islamic traditions by using the term <u>According to the Quran</u>.
- Islamic tradition teaches that their hero, the Prophet

Muhammed, was illiterate and was taught the information contain in the Koran by the Archangel Djabrail or Gabriel and that he retain the entire Koran by memory. This tradition goes on to say that the Prophet Muhammed dictated the entire Koran from memory to a scribe. Question: who and what is the Archangel Gabriel? In order for me to answer this question I will have to first introduce you to the Archangel Israfil. By Islamic tradition Israfil was supposedly the teacher of the archangel Gabriel. I will quote from the Shorter Encyclopedia of Islam to do so. "Israfil, the name of an Archangel, which is probably to be traced back to the Hebrew Serafim as is indicated by the variants Sarafil and Sarafin (TA, vii 375). The change of liquids is not unusual in such endings. His size is astounding; while his feet are under the seventh earth, his head reaches up to the pillars of the divine throne. He has four wings; one in the west, one in the east, one with which he covers his body and one as a protection against the majesty of God. He is covered with hair, mouths, and tongues. He is considered to be the angel who reads out the divine decisions from the well kept tablet and transmit them to the Archangel to whose department they belong. Three times by day and three by night he looks down into hell and is convulsed with grief and weeps so violently that the earth might be inundated by his tears. For three years he was the companion of the

Prophet, whom he initiated into the work of a prophet. Gabriel then took over this task and began the communication of the Kur'an. Alexander is said to have met him before his arrival in the land of darkness; there he stood upon a hill and blew the trumpet, tears in his eyes. If he is called Lord of the trumpet, it is mainly because he continually holds the trumpet to his mouth in order to be able to blow at once as soon as god gives the order for the blast which is to arouse men from their graves. It is however also said that Israfil will be first aroused on the day of the resurrection. He will then take his stand upon the Holy Rock in Jerusalem and give the signal which will bring the dead back to life. In modern Egypt, it is said that his music will refresh the inhabitants of paradise."

I will now introduce you to the Archangel Gabriel who according to Islamic tradition taught the Prophet Muhammed the Kur'an. I will now quote from the Shorter Encyclopedia of Islam, "Djabrail, or Djibril, Gabriel, is the best known figure among the angels of Islam. He is one of the four archangels, favoured by or brought near 'God, and one of the divine messengers. His duty is to bear the orders of God to mortal Prophets and to reveal his mysteries to them.

The name as well as the function has been taken over from Jewish and Christian religious tradition also the art. Gabriel plays an important part in the Kur'an; Muhammed applied the legend of this celestial messenger holding converse with the Prophets to himself and believed that he had received his mission and the subject of his preaching from him. Gabriel's name only appears three times in the Kur'an; but in other and important passages, a certain personage is designated by titles or epithets such as "The Spirit," "The Terrible," or even quite indirectly, and the commentators unanimously recognize Gabriel in this personage. This identification is quite justified by a comparison of the different passages. It is possible that Muhammed did not give a name at once to the spirit with which he felt himself possessed, as the three passages in which Gabriel's name appears are late (ii, 97 SQ.;ixvi, 4). In Sura xcvi, which in all probability is connected with the first revelation of the spirit and the crisis in which he received his mission, the angel is not designated by any name or title; the account, which is quite brief and perhaps mutilated, is impersonal; there it is said: "Recite in the name of thy Lord who has created;...recite, for thy Lord is the most beneficent."

According to tradition, this first revelation took place on Mount Hira' near Mecca, whither Muhammed had retired, and the voice is said to have added: "O Muhammed, thou art the apostle of God, and I am Gabriel." But this may be only a later development, inspired by I 19 of the Gospel of St. Luke, where the angel says to Zacharias: "I am Gabriel, that stand in the presence of God: and I am sent to speak unto thee and to show thee these glad tidings."

It appears that as a rule Muhammed heard the spirit, but did not see him. Indeed, there are verses in Sura Liii, (1-18) written with great vigor and a deep feeling of sincerity from which it is clear that he only saw him on two occasions: "It is one mighty in power that has taught him; it is the vigorous one; he hovered in the loftiest sphere, then he came down and remained suspended in the air. He was at a distance of two bows' length or nearer still; and he revealed to the servant of god, what he had to reveal to him...He had already seen him in another vision near the lote tree that marks the boundary...the lote tree was all covered." The minuteness of the details leaves no room to doubt the sincerity of the visionary. Tradition adds that after this vision, Gabriel brought to the Prophet the mare or Chimaera Burak (q.v.). The legend of the Archangel Gabriel is highly developed among Muslims; this is soon noticed if one looks through works rich in legends. There is scarcely a prophet to whom this celestial envoy has not brought help or revelations.

Gabriel consoled Adam after the fall and revealed to him twenty-one leaves; he taught him the cultivation of wheat, the working of iron and letters of the alphabet. He took him to the site of Mecca where he taught him the rites of pilgrimage. It was Gabriel also who showed Noah how to build the ark; he saved Abraham from the flames (cf. Sura xxi-69) and had many further relations with the Patriarch. He helped Moses to fight against the magicians of Egypt and at the exodus he appeared on a horse with white feet to deceive the Egyptians to enter the Red Sea, which was to swallow them up. He appeared to Samuel, and to David to whom he taught the art of making coats of mail; He comforted this prophet and brought him leaves with ten riddles that Solomon solved. As in the Gospel, he came to Zacharias to announce the birth of St. John. In the preparation of charms and talismans, Gabriel also plays an important part; his name frequently appears on the sides of magic squares, for example, along with those of the other archangels, Mika'il, Azra'il, and Israfil."

What you have just read concerning Israfil and the Archangel Gabriel is what traditional Islam teaches the Muslims in the Islamic community worldwide, and the Moslems believe these mythical stories wholeheartedly without question. Again, this proves the dominant Jewish and Christian influence that is so glaring in the make up of Islam and the Koran.

I want to reiterate and remind you that the archangel Israfil is a monster that is covered with hair including his mouths and tongues which indicate this mythical monster has more than one mouth and tongue. Also, I want to bring to your attention that the Archangel Gabriel is a little bird. This little celestial bird as the story goes came in contact with Adam, Abraham, and Isma'il, Moses, David, Samuel, Solomon, and Egyptians at the mythical biblical Exodus. In the gospels he came to Zacharias to announce the birth of St. John, but the most important of all for the Muslims is that he dictated the entire Quran to the illiterate Prophet Muhammed, thereby causing the Muhammedan religion to be changed to Islam.

One of the definitions for the word Islam is 'a teaching based on Muhammed 'as written in the Koran. This Islamic tradition causes Gabriel to be highly respected throughout the Islamic world. Think of all the Muslims throughout the Islamic world who believe in these childish mythological stories.

- The archangel Gabriel and Israfil come from Jewish and Christian literature. Without these two bodies of literature, there would be no Koran, as we know it today.
- It is commonly known among most scholars that the Koran contains two bodies of literature. One from Jewish writings called the Pentateuch and Psalms (Pirke Aboth) and the second comes from Christian writings known as the Four Gospels (Patristic Theology).
- Question: How can the Archangel Gabriel teach the entire Koran to the Prophet Muhammed in the 7th century when the religion called Judaism was non-existent? Additionally, the religion called Christianity had no written or printed literature until the 16th century (1516) when Desiderius Erasmus created the Synoptic Gospels. As you continue to read, the supporting reasons will be presented.
- Every religion has a beginning or a genesis. Judaism,

contrary to tradition was the last of the three major western religions to be created. However, Judaism was the first of the three religions to print religious literature, which was the Hebrew Bible in 1475 in Bologna, Italy. This is how Judaism merited the position of first when indeed its development was the third or last to be created. Serapis/Christianity was the first. The second was Monophysitism based on a doctrine derived from Arianism, a doctrine concerning the human nature of Serapis/Christ. See *The Historical Origin of Christianity*, Chapter II.

A second reason why tradition teaches that Judaism was the first and oldest religion is that the created Jesus the Christ was portrayed as a Jew in the fourth Gospel, John. Christian tradition teaches that after the death of this Jesus came Christianity, which is purported to be the second religion. However, this traditional teaching is historically incorrect. Judaism cannot predate the Baron Solomon Bar Isaac called RASHI (1040-1105) or Moses Maimonides (1135-1204). Also, Judaism cannot predate the first Crusade of 1096. Judaism is not a B.C. religion. As previously stated, Judaism was the first to produce printed religious literature. This came about in 1475 when the world's first printed Bible, called the Hebrew Bible, was printed for the Christian Community in Bologna, Italy under capitalistic influence. During this time in world history, the Capitalists had control of the first printing press in Europe with moveable type, built by Johann Gutenberg in 1437 in Germany. As a result of the Old Testament being printed in 1475 for the Christian community, this left the Roman Catholic Christian community in Europe without any printed literature or a Bible for and about their religious object "Jesus the Christ." To fulfill this void, Pope Alexander VI (1492-1503) in 1500 commissioned the playwright and ex-priest Desiderius Erasmus (1466?-1536) to write something on the object of Christianity or Christ.

Erasmus created and propounded the world's first New Testament and second Bible, The Novum Instrumentum, a.k.a., the Synoptic Gospels (Mark, Matthew, and Luke), that were first printed in 1516 by the Froben Press in Basil, Switzerland. The Novuum Instrumentum was changed and called the Novuum Testamentum in 1519 and changed again in 1535 to its permanent name The New Testament. These three gospels were the first of the biblical gospels to be published. Ninety-five years later the fourth gospel, John, was created and published in the King James Bible. A Bible created and dedicated to King James I of England in 1611 by Lancelot Andrewes, an English Theologian who selected other theologians to help create the so-called Authorized Version.

- After learning and realizing these facts about the Koran, how can the Islamic world and Muslims accept the tradition that the Archangel Gabriel taught the Prophet Muhammed the entire Koran?

- Islamic tradition teaches that the Prophet Muhammed was born in 570 A.D. and died in 632 A.D. What you have just read will assist you in realizing that The Old and New Testaments were unthinkable in 570 or 632 A. D. However, today these writings are the base foundation of the Koran and Islam.

Again, I reiterate that according to Orthodox. traditional Islamic teachings, it is against Islamic law to display any icons or images of the Prophet Muhammed. However, when there is a depiction of Muhammed, it is usually an image without a face. It is a faceless Muhammed without a mouth, eyes, or ears. Question: If the image of Muhammed is faceless (see front cover of this book), how could the Archangel Gabriel teach this icon that has no ears to hear the entire Qu'ran? If Muhammed had no face, he had no mouth to speak with. Therefore, how could this icon dictate by memory the entire Qu'ran to a scribe? The description of a faceless icon of Muhammed is indicative of a non-human object. Who gives the Bible or the Qu'ran authority? Answer: The Christians or Muslims by believing in it.

In this section of the book, I want to bring to your attention that there is no one single language or dialect that can be identified or called Arabic today. There are many different dialects spoken in various countries throughout the Arab Islamic world. The first group to bring a dominant change of language to North and Northeast Africa, including Egypt, intentionally called the Middle East, were the Seljuk Turks who erupted out of Iran in 1071-79 and over ran their brethren the Saracen Arabs. The Saracens who were Monophysites lived throughout the aforementioned land areas in Africa during this time. This eruption by the Turks also threatened the Byzantine Emperors and their empire in 1071. At this time Greek was the dominant language. The Seljukian Turks originally came from the Turkestan area of Southern Russia and from Afghanistan into Iran. They brought with them a Turkic language dialect that provided the foundation of what is currently called Arabic. This language began to dissipate the Greek language spoken throughout the Byzantine Empire.

Arabic dialects were used even more when the Ottoman Turks began to topple the Byzantine Empire in 1300 and took control of their land holdings. Today some of the people living in the so-called middle east (Northeast Africa) and North Africa and beyond cannot communicate verbally with each other. However, they are able to understand each other if what they want to say is written using the classical Arabic Script.

Use of the Arabic script helped the learned Arabs in the Muhammedan communities to unify themselves when the Koran was accepted by the Muhammedan world in 1919 in Cairo, Egypt. The questions must be asked what is the Arabic alphabet? And, where did it come from? Who created and developed this alphabet? I will begin by stating that the Arabs never had a script or an alphabet. During the time of antiquity an African people living in the Continent of Africa who are known to the world today as the Ancient Egyptians were the only people who were literate. The rest of the world populous was illiterate. This included the Greeks and the Romans. It is important to our understanding when studying the alphabet to know that every alphabet had its beginning in Ancient Egypt. The Ancient Egyptians developed a system of writing that was one of their greatest achievements. (See alphabet chart on page 132) The Ancient Egyptians developed three forms of written communications; the first form was pictorial drawings or hieroglyphs. The second and third forms are the Phonetic I and Phonetic II alphabets respectively that allowed the Ancient Egyptians to write by the sound of what was spoken. The European academic community starting with James Bruce in the 1760's has designated the Phonetic I and Phonetic II alphabets of the Ancient Egyptians to be called Hieratic and Demotic. These two scripts are known today as the Arabic script. The old Phonetic I and Phonetic II are written in calligraphy with modern adaptations. From the Ancient Egyptian Phonetic alphabets came the Greek, Latin, Hebrew, and Arabic scripts, which are all misnomers. Getting back to the so-called Arabic script, today this script has 28 letters, which are two more characters than used in English. All the letters represent consonants. Vowels are indicated by marks above and below the letters. Arabic is written from right to left, rather than from left to right. The Arabic alphabet contains 18 letter shapes, however, by adding one, two, or three dots to letters with similar Phonetic characters a total of 28 letters is obtained. Long vowels are included, while diacritics can be added to indicate short vowels.

The Phonetic I and Phonetic II scripts of the Ancient Egyptians were also used as a form of art and architectural art by the Coptic Monophysite and Melchite Egyptian Africans called Moors in Spain. This is evidenced by the cities they built such as Granada, Cordoba, Seville, and others starting in the mid- eleventh century. After the rise of Islam in the early 20th century, use of the Phonetic I and the Phonetic II alphabets spread rapidly especially in the Koran. The main two families of the so-called Arabic alphabet were the calligraphic styles called generally the Kufic and the soft cursive styles which include Naskhi, Thuluth, Nastalaq, and many others. Since several letters of the Arabic alphabet share the same shapes and since vowels are not clearly indicated, some reform was needed to avoid confusion. A system of letters pointing (NAQT or Ijam) and vowel indication (Taskell) were developed. In the 11th century the Hieratic-Demotic or Phonetic I and Phonetic II letters began to be modified and used as ornaments and new geometric elements started to appear in the form of plaiting, knotting, and braiding. The exaggerated use of such ornaments created complex compositions, which were difficult to decipher at times.

During the 13th and 14th centuries, square Kufic developed out of the use of calligraphy in buildings all over the major cities of Spain, Cordoba, Granada, Seville, etc. It was used to cover entire buildings, a practice unique to the African builders called Moors who brought civilization to pagan Spain beginning in 1051. The shape of each letter depends on its position in a word—initial, medical, and final. Another practice unique to the African builders in Spain during this time.

There is a fourth form of letters when written alone has certain significant values. The letters alif, waw, and ya (standing for glottal stop, w, and y respectively) are used to represent the long vowels a, u, and i. A set of diacritical marks are sometimes used to represent short vowels and certain grammatical endings otherwise left unmarked.

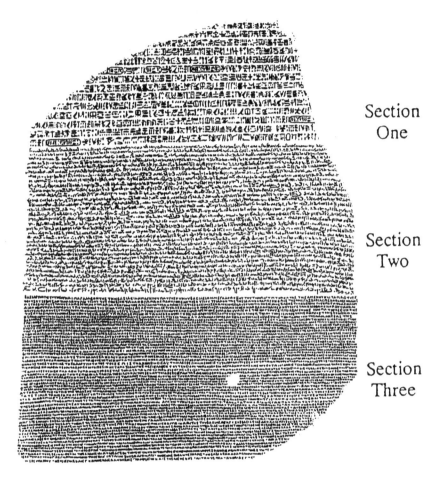

The Rosetta Stone showing the three forms of writings of the Ancient Egyptians: Section one-The Medu Netcher or Hieroglyphics, Section Two-The Phonetic Alphabet #one a.k.a., Hieratic Demotic, and Section Three-The Phonetic Alphabet #two an expansion of Phonetic #1. Both the Phonetic #one and #two are today misnomers and called the Arabic Script, Hebrew and Greek/Latin alphabets.

Things to Think About Outside Islamic Tradition

	EGYPTIAN			GREEK				LATIN			HE-BREW
1	𓅃	Z	ꓘ	A	A	λ	α	A	A	λαa	א
2				B	B	β	B	B	Bb		ב
3		Z	7	7	Γ	Γ	⌐Y	⟨	C	⟨Cᴄᴄꟈ	ℷ
4			Δ	Δ	Δ	Δ	δ	Ɗ	D	ẟẟd	ᴛ
5					E	e	ε	ϝ	E	ee	ה
6			५	५	YF		ℱ	ϝ	F	ℱf	ו
7		ℒ	ꓲ	ꓲ	I	Ż	ℨℭ	ℐ	Z	z	ℸ
8			⊟	⊟	H	H	h η	⊟	H	hh	⊓
9			⊕	⊕	⊙	Θ	θ ϑ	⊗		.	ט
10	\\	५	ꓘ	ꓘ	I	I	ι	I	I	ij	י
11				ꓱ	K	K	κ ϰ	K	K	k	ℶ
12		ℒ	ℓ	∨	⋀	λ	λ	ℒ	L	ℓl	ℷ
13		ℨ	ꓵ	M	M	M	μμ	M	M	ᴍ m	ℳ
14				ꓵ	N	N	ν ϒ	N	N	n n	ℶ
15			‡	‡	Ξ	ℨ	ξ	⊞	+	x x	℺
16			o	o	O	O	o	O			ע
17			ꓶ	Γ	Π	π ϖ	P	P	P		פ
18			Γ	Γ	M		ꙃ	Γ			צ
19			φ	φ	φ	Q			Q	qq	ꞝ
20			ꝗ	ꝗ	P	P	ϱ P	ℙ	R	ꝝꝝ	ר
21			w	ℨ	ℨ	C	⊏ σ	ꟻ	S	∫∫s	ש
22			‡	Ꞇ	T	T	τ	T	T	ℯ t	ת
	i	ii	iii	iv	v	vi	vii	viii	ix	x	xi

Alphabet Chart

The world's first system of writing by the Ancient Egyptians:
Column 1-The Medu-Netcher-Hieroglyphics, Column 2-Hieratic
Phonetic I, and Column 3-The Phonetic II.   From the two
Phoenetic Ancient Egyptian Alphabets come the misnomers of the
Greek/Latin and Arabic/Hebrew Alphabets.

- The supposed Arabic alphabet became the language of the Koran. When one hears the term "The Arabic Language," it is referring to the Arabic script as being the language and not speech or spoken words.

- The Arabic script was changed in Turkey by its new President, Mustafa Kemal, known as Ataturk (1923-1938) who became President of the Turkish Republic in 1923 with the help of the British and the French. He decided in 1928 that the Ancient Egyptian script that is referred to as the misnomer, Arabic Script, which had been used by the African Coptic Community for centuries, should be replaced with a Roman Latin alphabet. Ataturk had realized the Arabic script was ill suited for the many different Turkish dialects spoken in Turkey. By using the so-called Latin alphabet with its 29 letters (eight vowels and 21 consonants), he would eliminate the complexities of the Arabic script. This reform enabled children and adults to read and write within a few months, and to study western languages with greater effectiveness. This also helped Ataturk to reform Turkey from its old Ottoman Turkish way of life to a westernized European culture in which he added the use of the Gregorian Calendar, the metric system, and westernized civil and criminal laws. In 1934 every Turk had to choose a surname for himself. He then went on to cast aside the harem, veil, and fez.

Note: All that you have read should provide some in-sight about the so-called Arabic script/language.

- Question: Where did Islam get its name? In the Family and Table of Nations written in the Old Testament Bible, the descendants of Adam leads to Noah, who has a son, named Shem. The descendants of Shem are traced to Abraham. It was the willing submission of Abraham in the supreme test to obey God in the attempted sacrifice of his son Isaac. This story also is described in the Koran by the verb, "Aslama," which provided Islam its name.

- Question: If there were Biblical and Koranic characters such as Adam, Eve, Noah, Shem. Abraham, Ishmael, and Hagar, for example, where are the burial or shrine sites for these religious named characters? Why are pilgrimages not made to and for these world famous religious characters?

- Question: According to traditional Islamic teachings, the Prophet Muhammed died and was buried in Madina in 632 and ascended into heaven from Madina on the date of his death. Also, Islamic tradition teaches that Muhammed ascended into heaven from the Dome of the Rock Mosque in Jerusalem on the date of death. How can this prophet Muhammed ascend into heaven from two different land areas at the same time, especially when the supposed Holy Land (Jerusalem) where the Dome of the Rock Mosque was built is only slightly over a hundred years old?

Take note of the following:
- There is no recorded biography or data for a birth of a Prophet Muhammed of tradition being born in Mecca. So the question has to be asked where was this Prophet Muhammed born? Again, see the "Shorter Encyclopedia of Islam" for more details.

- In The Columbia Encyclopedia, second edition 1950-56 on the subject of the Negro, it says "Mohammadanism has won many converts and Christianity some adherents."

- In a speech in New York City around 1917 the Black Nationalist Marcus Garvey said "The Negro practices two religions, "Mohammadanism and Christianity."

- In both The Columbia Encyclopedia and the speech by Marcus Garvey, Islam was not used, instead Mohammadanism was used.

- Think about this statement, "To date the religion called Islam is less than 100 years old. Islam will be 89 years old in the year 2008 counting from the completion and acceptance of the Koran in 1919 by the Arab World in Cairo, Egypt.

- Another very important piece of information I want to bring to your attention is about the word and term "Sura," which is used in the Koran to mean "chapters." This term came from Jewish scholars who influenced and helped develop the Koran and the religion called Islam. I will quote from the Encyclopedia Dictionary of Judaism. "Sura, site of a leading Babylonian academy. Main center of Torah learning for most of the period between 3rd and early 5th centuries and in the 8th – 10th centuries when the academy was transferred to Baghdad." So, as one can see even the term Sura came from Jewish Pirke Avot (Aboth) fiction. After considering all that you have read, I want you the reader to think about the information that I have provided and use your analytical mind to think about this information. At this point, you may begin to realize that Islam along with Christianity and Judaism is all based on mythology and not facts. Using the words of the Great Malcolm X we have been " bamboozled."

CHAPTER IX

WHAT HAPPENED TO THE CHURCH OF
HAGIA SOPHIA?
A Connection between Christianity and Islam

The Church of Hagia Sophia often referred to as the Great Church is considered the largest and most important surviving church of antiquity. This author would add and the oldest built church. Hagia Sophia marked the beginning of religious traditions that continued for almost 1400 years as well as provided an architectural prototype for churches, mosques, synagogues, and government buildings. Some may ask why devote an entire chapter to this one edifice, the Hagia Sophia, known as the Church of the Holy Wisdom and St. Sophia.

The Hagia Sophia was and is more than an edifice. It is the first seat or See of Christianity. It possesses its own unique history. It is a marvel that preceded the Vatican in the West by almost 1000 years. It is located on the continent of Africa in Istanbul, Turkey (Constantinople of antiquity). Its rich history holds the possibilities of teaching everyone something, particularly those persons who are not familiar with its significance or in some cases its existence. Although it still stands in all of its magnificence, its significance has been minimized, masked, camouflaged, at the very least ignored. Yet its influence is ubiquitous. It is everywhere.

The time has come for people in the religious world in

particular and others in general to recognize consciously a common history that binds us together. Lies, greed, and distortions that have torn the people of the world apart and continue to rip at hearts and force nations into war also must be brought into the light. Too many human lives have perished and continue to perish in wars and so-called peacekeeping efforts without the participants or observers understanding why or the history of the religious underpinnings of the wars in which our men and women fight. It is estimated that 300,000 or more persons die every five years due to what is often an ages old religious ancestral conflict.

In America some have said that the envy of America and the wealth of the west are the primary causes of America's conflict with the rest of the world. Others say that it is the arrogance and policies of America that favor and support one religion over another. And yet another might say that it is religion and all of its rituals, customs, self-righteous attitude of possessing the only "truth" and the exercise of power that can accompany such thinking undergirded by military might. Each point has some merit, however, the latter is something that we cannot ignore or dismiss easily. It deserves a closer look. Religion by its very nature is divisive and competitive and rooted in intolerance and arrogance. The evidence is apparent by the major divisions, denominations, sub-divisions, and sects, and factions within each religion.

The Church of Hagia Sophia is relevant to the history that brought the world to this point politically and religiously. In spite of all of its glory, magnificence, and important role in history and organized religion, very few have ever heard of this structure as a Church, Mosque, Museum, or simply as an extraordinary architectural accomplishment unless one has been fortunate enough to travel to Turkey. With the exception of the Great Pyramid complex and temples of Ancient Egypt, this is one of the greatest architectural fetes of all times. To look at the Hagia Sophia is to look at a part of the history of Orthodox Eastern Byzantine Christianity, Monophysite Christianity and Muhammedanism/Islam, and the havoc that each has wrought, beginning with the created Serapis/Christ image in Ancient Egypt.

Equally as amazing, if not more amazing is the fact that The Church of Hagia Sophia is the world's first official seat of Christianity and the first Christian Church built for and exclusively dedicated to the worship of the Christ image. Certainly temples were converted for the worship of Serapis (forerunner of Christ) and Isis and other deities for example, but again not built initially with the sole purpose in mind of honoring the created Christ. Even so, the Church of Hagia Sophia never is referenced as the first seat of Christianity or acknowledged for its unique position in Christianity and Muhammedanism or Islamic history with the known exception of Walter Williams in his book, *The Historical Origin of*

Christianity. Before proceeding it is important for informational purposes to note that most sources on the Hagia Sophia indicate that there were two previous Churches of Hagia Sophia built on the same location as the present structure. In a report received from the Turkish Embassy it refers to a <u>legendary</u> history that began in 326 during the reign of Constantine I. If this were the case, why would Constantine continue to build pagan temples to other sun gods as history indicates? The hippodrome served as his axis of the Byzantine world and not the Church of Hagia Sophia. Is there any significance in this? From Justinian's period forward (527-565) the Church of Hagia Sophia was the jewel of the Byzantine Empire. The information from the Embassy also states that some historians claim that the first building was begun by Constance, son of Constantinus, and opened to the public by Constantinus II. This first structure was supposedly called Megali Ecclesia, due to its size and later called "The Sophia". Since the 5th century, it has been known as Hagia Sophia, which means Divine Wisdom. Depending on the reference, the same is said of the third or current Hagia Sophia. The first edifice was to have burned down in June 404 during the reign of Emperor Arcadius, which was supposedly due to the exile of the Patriarch of Constantinople, John Chrysostom. This author has observed over time that when information presented as fact is questionable, the information that follows is confused, contradictory, and conflicted. In contrast, when information is provable and clear evidence exists and can be deemed a fact, it is consistent, clear, it rings true within a person and it fits within a historical context.

The second Hagia Sophia was rebuilt supposedly during the period of Theodosius II and reopened October 10, 415. Very little is known about the architecture of this building just as little is known about the first structure. This second structure supposedly burned down along with some other buildings during the Nika Riot, a battle between the Blues and Greens against the rule of the Byzantine Emperor Justinian, on the 13 of January 532. This writer does not embrace these overlapping traditional stories coming from the Turkish Embassy or the present pseudo history that purports that a Christian Church existed prior to the Council of Ephesus, convoked in 431. This must be repudiated because history does not support the existence of a Jesus Christ in human form. History supports that the Christ and the Virgin Mary were created and agreed upon at the Council of Ephesus in 431. The close of the Council of Chalcedon in 451 marked the official beginning of Christianity. Any religious structure prior to Ephesus and Chalcedon most likely was used in the worship of Serapis, Isis, Osiris, and or other Sun gods. For more details, see Williams' *Historical Origin of Christianity*. I will leave the reader to ponder this along with the predating of a Christ, Christianity, or the building of the world's first Christian Church in 532 by Emperor Justinian prior to the Councils of Ephesus and Chalcedon.

While the Hagia Sophia is considered one of the most brilliant architectural fetes ever achieved under European rule although built and designed by Africans, few in the West seem to be familiar with the Church of Hagia Sophia. Let's take a closer look at the background of this marvel.

Emperor Justinian and his wife Theodora commissioned the building of the Hagia Sophia in which construction of the See (church) began in 532. The edifice was completed five years later in 537. Today the Church of Hagia Sophia is hailed as the supreme example of Byzantine era architecture. Here is what the historian Procopius (d 562) said of the Hagia Sophia:

"The Church is distinguished by indescribable beauty, excelling both in the harmony of its measures, having no part excessive and none deficient; being more magnificent than ordinary buildings, and much more elegant than those which are not of so just a proportion. The church is singularly, full of light and sunshine; you would declare that the place is not lighted by the sun from without, but that the rays are produced within itself, such an abundance of light is poured into this church..." and "men rejoice in what they see."

The Hagia Sophia was the centerpiece of the 'Queen of Cities' or Constantinople, Turkey, the capital of the Roman Byzantine Empire located on the African continent with a small section bordering Europe along the Bosporus. Emperor Justinian dedicated his pride and joy, the Church, on Sunday, December 27, 537. And he consecrated it to what he considered the one god, Christ, that possessed the attributes of the Ancient Egyptian god Osiris, and called it the Hagia Sophia. The name means Holy Wisdom, which is another name for Christ. Erroneously, the Church is often referred to as St. Sophia.

In Justinian's vision, Hagia Sophia symbolized the hope for unification of his Empire following the many years of strife and debate that caused the first four historical Ecumenical Council meetings to take place over several centuries. The struggle actually began with the rule of Alexander, the Macedonian, when he went into Ancient Egypt and wanted to become a part of the sacred priest society and desired to be worshipped. He was under the mistaken impression that Pharaohs were worshipped and that was what accounted for the glorious civilization and orderly society that existed in Ancient Egypt. Probably more significant, he quickly became aware that in order to be a legitimate ruler of Ancient Egypt he had to sit on the throne of Isis and be accepted by the sacred Priest society. After failing to be accepted in the sacred priest society, Alexander died nine years later in 323 B.C. without realizing his goal. He was succeeded in Egypt by one of his army generals, Ptolemy I Lagi, called Soter (Savior) who also tried to get his "image" accepted and worshipped.

Ptolemy I later located a group of priest and priestesses in Memphis, Egypt to admit him into their society. For more information on this topic, see Walter Williams' *The Historical Origin of Christianity*. Williams provides an outstanding treatise on Alexander, Ptolomies, and the Coptics and their roles though not always honorable and the Ecumenical Council Meetings. Chronologically he presents the many polemics or arguments between the Dyophysites, Monophysites, Nestorians, and Arianists regarding the image of Ptolemy I who was given the name O'Serapis, then Serapis that later became the Christ. You will find it fascinating.

It is important to note that it was some of the direct descendants of the Ancient Egyptians, the Melchite Copts, who played a major role in establishing the Hagia Sophia. They not only designed and built the structure dedicated to the image of Christ, the Melchite Copts created the first homilies or sermons years before the Hagia Sophia was built. Homilies that were first created in the latter part of the fourth century to honor the forerunner of Christ, Serapis, that had been created in 320 B.C. They were later used to anchor the Church and, perhaps, made applicable to the Christ. John Chrysostom (c347-407), the African Melchite Copt, is considered the father of homilies. However, his homilies were not homilies concerning Christ, but homilies concerning Serapis the predecessor of Christ. His homilies were later switched and applied to the Christ in the Church of Hagia Sophia.

Today, he is recognized by the Roman Catholic Church as a Doctor of the Church and is given recognition for creating homilies. John Chrysostom's homilies are used today by other Eastern and Western Christian Churches throughout the world and are considered the most beautiful ever produced. His writings concerning the priesthood are held in the highest esteem and remain in continuous use. The Roman Catholic Church celebrates all saints holiday that is held annually in honor of John or St. John.

Again, Copts were the designers and builders of this wonderful structure that surely must have reminded them of the work of their ancestors of Ancient Egypt who inspired their work.

John Chrysostom

John Chrysostom today referred to as St. John, the Father of Homilies. Scene is from a wall painted tile that is part of an eleventh century mosaic miniature in the Church of Hagia Sophia. Observe the African features and hair.

Justinian held on to his vision of the Church of Hagia Sophia being the axis of his empire and a symbol of unity and peace. The Great Church building itself was to be a part of this grand plan. Justinian and Theodora continued to try to realize the dream of a United Empire just as Constantine had dreamed. Justinian and Theodora made a gallant effort to bring the polemic between the Dyophysitic Copts and the Monophysite Copts to a close or at least a compromised understanding. The Dyophysitics embraced the idea that Christ had a human nature as well as a divine Osiris like spirit and the Monophysites embraced the one nature of the created Christ, the divine-Osiris like spirit. Thus the Monophysites refused to accept that it possessed a human nature because they had a living memory of the events that led to its creation. In a further effort to bring about unity, Justinian and Theodora appointed Patriarchs to represent the Dyophysitic and Monophysitic factions respectively. They housed and accommodated both factions in the Hagia Sophia although the Church was officially Dyophysitic Christian or Orthodox Chalcedonian, accepting Christ's perfection as god and man. Further, two offices were established, The Patriachate of Hagia Sophia or Great Church represented the Dyophysitics and the West (Rome) primarily. They also established the Patriarchate of Constantinople, which represented the Monophysites or the East (Egypt, Ethiopia, and Syria). Of course, this arrangement also made it easy for the Emperor and Empress to watch over both factions and have control over them and deal with their own internal conflicts regarding their personal preferences. Nonetheless, Justinian as the personification of Orthodoxy was tied theologically and politically to the West.

For over nine centuries or 900 years, the Church of Hagia Sophia stood in Turkey on the Continent of Africa as the seat of the Christian world and as the First University for Europeans, staffed by Africans as teachers. Take note of the fact that Turkey was one of the countries during the time of antiquity that was part of the African Continent before the world was remapped and names changed. A celebration was held yearly on each anniversary of the Church of Hagia Sophia for 900 plus years until the seat of Christianity was moved to Europe in the 15th Century (1445). A Mass for Christ marked the celebrations or Christ Mas(s), today shortened to Christmas. Today the Roman Catholic Church is given credit for popularizing Christmas or do they mean December 25th, for there were many Masses held in honor of Christ on other dates throughout history. But, in Europe December 25th was the date on which other Sun gods were worshipped, close to Winter Solstice and the New Year.

Note that December 25th was well established in the West as a day dedicated to the worship of sun gods, and it was usurped by the Catholic Church after the seat of

Christianity moved to the West (Rome). competing with the worship of other images and other gods in their midst. However, the Roman Catholic Church only worshipped Christ as their 'son' god on December 25th. This was a ritual carried over from the Church of Hagia Sophia that celebrated the birth of the Church and Christ on the same date of December 27th, 537 for over 900 years until the seat was moved to Europe (Rome-The Vatican) in 1445. The difference of two days was ignored to coincide with the worship of the other established gods in Rome. So, today the Mas(s) for Christ is celebrated on December 25th, and is called Christmas and the Hagia Sophia is discounted.

Masses for the image began in Egypt with the celebration called the Epiphany during the time of the Ptolemy rule of Egypt. This celebration originally gave honor to Serapis and the Ptolomies who were the vicars of Serapis. Later Serapis became the Christ at the Council of Ephesus in 431. Today this celebration is still being practiced from December 26 to January 6 by some Eastern Orthodox Churches that do not celebrate the Christ Mass on December 25th. It is known today as the Epiphany or little Christ-mass.

To reiterate, if we are ever to have peace, it must begin with Truth/facts. Ironically there was very little peace in and around the Church of Hagia Sophia. There were on going conflicts and uprisings. While, the history of the Hagia Sophia has the possibilities of representing a truth or fact that has virtually disappeared over time. It is part of a past that has been ignored. It is inconceivable that history of this magnitude has not been given its place of importance in the development of Dyophysitic Christianity and Monophysitism turned Muhammedanism/Islam and hailed as one of the Wonders of the World. As with the Pyramids, we can see it, visit it, touch it, and physically behold it because it is real and still stands today. Many of the other so-called Wonders are gone and questions of whether some ever existed have been raised and continue to be raised. Interestingly, these formidable enduring structures, the Great Pyramid and Church of Hagia Sophia are located in Africa and were built by the Ancient Egyptian Africans and their direct descendants, the African Coptic Egyptians.

Perhaps, it is redundant to restate that it is incomprehensible and downright disturbing how the Church of Hagia Sophia that symbolized the first seat of Christianity from 537 until 1453 could be ignored or omitted from Western history. It is troublesome. This is strikingly analogous to the achievements of the people of African descent being ignored and left out of the history books of the West. Sometimes they are disguised as some other race, group, renamed, and or worse identities and achievements stolen. Clearly an attempt to dehumanize and justify the degrading treatment of a people. Consequently, everyone has been cheated and the world is worse off because of it. Could there be much more to conceal about the Hagia (Aya) Sophia?

The Church of Hagia Sophia has more significance, its location. It is located in Constantinople, today Istanbul, Turkey, which was located on the Continent of Africa before the world was politically remapped. The mention of Turkey seems innocent enough. However, what is less straightforward is that Turkey is located in Northeast Africa. It is repeatedly placed in Europe or Southwest Asia and identified as the Middle East much like Egypt and other countries in Northeast Africa, such as Syria, Jordan, Lebanon, illegal state of Israel, Palestine, Arabia, Iraq, Yemen, Iran, etc. Some of these lands also are named in the mythical Bible and Koran.

Our good common sense tells us that the Middle East is not an actual land area. It is a political term used to distort the real land area of Africa and its indigenous people. So many foreigners have occupied this area for so many centuries that its roots and indigenous people are often forgotten. Whether intentional, the results are the same. Moreover, given that Constantinople (modern Istanbul) was the capital of the Byzantine Eastern Roman Empire, this may lend itself to incorrect assumptions. The Church of Hagia Sophia was the nerve center and heart of the capital. It anchored the administrative complex of the Capital of the Eastern and Western Roman Byzantine Empire, which also had authority over the western portion of the Roman Empire. As we can see, the Roman Empire never fell, it merged under the name Byzantine. It did not fall in the true sense although it was under on-going seize. The seat of power changed just as it did in early America. Williamsburg, VA was the first capital, now it's Washington, D.C. The Emperor always had ecclesiastical and secular/political authority over the Church of Hagia Sophia. Thereby, making the Church and State one. They were synonymous. This began with the Emperor Justinian who took back the Donation of Constantine from the first Papa/ Pope or Bishop, Vigilus, in 555, which gave him the ecclesiastical authority. It was at that point that the Church and State became one. It appeared that Justinian felt that the Donation of Constantine in the hands of the Africans had achieved its purpose. The death of Vigilus marked the end of the ecclesiastical dominance and control of the Donation of Constantine in the hands of the African Papas. Although the Donation of Constantine came under the control of the Emperors, Africans continued to be appointed as Papas (Popes) or Patriarchs of the Hagia Sophia or Bishops of Rome. For many centuries the Byzantine Empire existed under on-going threats by usurpers from within and from the outside of the Empire.

The Church of Hagia Sophia remained the jewel. It was rich with symbolism, history, relics, and jewels literally and precious metals. It was the place where all Christians dreamed of making a pilgrimage. It was the Spiritual destination or "Holy Land," if you will for Christendom. There was no other. The Church of Hagia

Sophia was coveted throughout its history, including and during the time of the crusades. Religion and politics have distorted this truth.

The first serious threat or act of aggression that came to Hagia Sophia was with the emergence of the Saracens from within the Empire. Today they are referred to as the Saracen Islamic Arabs. They were the students of the African Copt, Jacob Baradea, who was appointed by Theodora in 543 to evangelize among the Europeans living in and around Constantinople after the Jacobite Church was built and the Nika riots were stopped. The Church was located in the area of Turkey that today is identified as Syria. The Jacobite Church was a Monophysite Church. The Jacobites embraced the ideology that the created Christ possessed an Osiris-like spirit only and no human nature. Theodora and Justinian exploited the religious differences. They used the Dyophysitic and Monophysitic argument for political purposes. It is said that on her deathbed Theodora asked her husband, Justinian, to take care of the Monophysite community.

Over the course of its history, the Byzantine Empire was usurped many many times by other Europeans who wished to control it, which resulted in many different rulers. Thus causing each Byzantine Emperors to be under constant danger from within and without of losing their political control and religious power over the Empire. The most serious threat to the Byzantine Empire came from the Seljukian Turks who erupted out of Iran in 1071 and from the Crusaders out of Europe, Italy, Germany, but mainly from France beginning in 1096-1099.

Note: The threat by the Seljuks against the Byzantine Empire was the reason for the Crusades to come about.

Erroneously, many historians have reported that the mission of the Crusaders was to protect pilgrims who were enroute to Jerusalem or to save Christianity. Their mission was not motivated by feelings of altruism to save Christianity, protecting Christian Pilgrims, or saving the Byzantine Empire although Christianity was used as a cloak to hide their main motivation, personal gain-greed of money and riches. One source refers to the Crusades as a Frankish enterprise because Barons financed their personal armies in which three out of four armies came from France. Their mission or job was to identify land opportunities for expansion and seizure through hook, crook, or murder. The greatest prize, the Church of Hagia Sophia including its riches was no exception.

Knowing of the real threats to his empire by the Seljukian Turks in 1095 Alexis I sought help from the West to fight off the Turkish "infidels." The likes of Peter the Hermit of France, Walter the Penniless from Germany along with other crusading armies financed by barons arrived at the gates of Constantinople. Alexis was looking for assistance. His goal was to recover the land lost to the Seljuks. He unwittingly and unknowingly and naively invited the enemies into his Empire.

This was far and away from the romantic picture of religious fervor that has been painted by so many historians writing on the subject of the Crusades. Alexius being somewhat wary required the Crusaders to take an oath that they would return the land that they recaptured from the Turks. Of course an oath or treaty is only as good as the integrity of the parties involved. This story reminds us of the numerous broken treaties throughout the history in this country between the government and the Indians and the promise of 40 acres and a mule to former slaves in America. Violation of this oath was no exception.

The enlightened historian Edward Gibbon understood that the first crusades in 1096 did not have a mission to secure the Holy Land. While the others plundered, the four baron armies usurped land and plundered countries. The army out of the north of France that was led by the bounty hunter and soldier Godfrey de Bouillon and his brother Baldwin seized the area that we know in modern times as Jerusalem in 1099. Thus the first Latin Kingdom of Jerusalem was established. Godfrey or GOD as his soldiers called him became the first Latin king. However, he relinquished his title to his brother, Baldwin I.

Legend has it that Godfrey visited and conferred with his financier the baron, RASHI, before launching his crusade. Solomon bar Isaac, called RASHI, is most known in history today as a Jewish commentator (inventor and contriver). RASHI is generally recognized as the person responsible for providing the foundation of Judaism. The world's Jewish community celebrated his 900th birthday in 1940. Is it possible that there is a connection between the land conquered by Godfrey's army in 1099 and the claims made that would ultimately resulted in the creation of the questionable state of Israel in 1948? Moreover, is this the basis of the wars that were fought in 1948, 1967, 1973, and today in the year 2002 over the same land area? The 1099 occupation lasted until Saladin conquered Jerusalem in 1187.

Note: The name Jerusalem is a modern biblical name and made part of the many myths, allegories, and metaphorical stories written in the Bible. During the Roman era Jerusalem was called "Aelia Capitolina." It was a part of a Roman colony founded and named by and for the Roman ruler Alelius Hadrianus, called "Hadrian" (117-138). There is absolutely no information other than the Bible that supports the notion that Jerusalem was a Holy Land. Maybe it was considered (w)holly owned by RASHI and or Godfrey and the descendant followers or Jews today since the first crusade was essentially a land grab.

In a perverse way the Seljuks indirectly saved Constantinople, the capital of the Byzantine Empire, from the Crusades and thus saved the Hagia Sophia from being stripped of its riches and possibly its legacy by the crusaders. See Chapter IV for more details on additional baron armies that fought in the first crusade and the lands usurped.

Once again, The Church of Hagia Sophia was "The Symbol" or home of Christianity and the place of Pilgrimage, not Jerusalem as claimed today. Jerusalem was not the home of Christianity. Today, based on the Bible, Jerusalem is considered to be a part of the state of Israel, divided between those who embrace Zionism and the religion, Judaism, and the Palestinians who embrace Islam. Neither group is indigenous to the area. If Judaism has a home, it probably would be Jerusalem according to the narrative stories in the Bible which was written by the Jews themselves who were dreaming, imagining, feeling entitled and unable to accept defeat, or those with other vested interests in making such claims. The question arises, was the Latin Kingdom of Jerusalem the beginning of this claim that is prompting the present day conflict which began in the late nineteenth century between the Palestinians and the believers in Zionism and Judaism, known today as Israelis?

The fourth crusade is credited with precipitating the decline of the eastern portion of the Roman Byzantine Empire. It was during this fourth crusade that commenced in 1204 that Constantinople was conquered by another French crusading army under the leadership of Baldwin II. For three days they looted the libraries and artifacts of the Church of Hagia Sophia, the envy of the world. The contents of the library included the writings of the Copts and their ancestors, the Ancient Egyptians. The crusaders took from the Hagia Sophia the most precious of relics that could not be procured for money in the ruder countries of Europe. The city was almost denuded of Christian relics and taken to Europe. Many artifacts that were absconded by the crusaders were later incorporated into the design of St. Mark Cathedral in Venice, Italy. The Cathedral today would not have its grandeur without the artifacts from the Great Church of Hagia Sophia. The jealousy, envy, and covetousness were appallingly destructive. There was probably much more to the destruction than we will ever know for sure, particularly if the relationship between the Hagia Sophia, St. Mark of Venice, and the Vatican were to be studied further. How did the Vatican acquire a Coptic Library and a Coptic Museum that they house if not from the Mother Church, Hagia Sophia? What is the interest? What other knowledge of our ancestors, the Ancient Egyptians, lies within?

Following the departure of the Latins and Venetians in 1261 after an almost bloodless coup, the Greeks were able to restore Constantinople to the Empire. Hagia Sophia remained the imperial church and the University at Hagia Sophia was refound. However, the City did not ever fully recover. Turmoil continued into the fourteenth century for what was left of the empire and Hagia Sophia.

The Church fell into disrepair and in 1433 a major earthquake caused severe cracks in its structure. This left the headquarters for the empire almost in ruins and the empire, reduced to Constantinople only, weak and vulnerable. The Seljuk Turks took advantage of the weakened state. However, the Seljuks soon gave way to their rivals - the Ottoman Turks. The Ottomans who had been around since the beginning of the fourteenth century established their capital at Adrianople, Turkey within twenty years. Their Sultanate surrounded Constantinople, except for the side that buttressed the Bosporus Sea. Near the end of the century the Byzantine Emperor was paying a protection fee to the Ottoman Sultan.

The fifteenth century marked another significant period in the history of the Church of Hagia Sophia and the Byzantine Empire. With the exception of Constantinople and its suburbs, the Byzantine Empire all but ended in 1439 at the Councils of Ferrara and Florence in Italy. Action taken by John VIII at these meetings signaled the beginning of the end. In his desperate attempt and last ditch effort to secure help from the West and preserve the Empire, John agreed to the Union of the Eastern and Western churches. It is important to clarify at this juncture that there was no Vatican in Rome in 1439. Development of the Vatican complex began in 1445 with the building of St. Peters Church in the suburbs of Rome over the catacombs. The building project would take 181 years (1626) to complete. Remember also that the seat of government for the Byzantine/Roman Empire resided in the East or Africa.

At the Council of Ferrara John VIII relinquished the

Donation of Constantine and the emblems that gave him his ecclesiastical authority. This signified the separation of Church and State and the imminent end of the Byzantine Empire and the transfer of the Seat (See) of Christianity or the office of the Vicar of Christ to the West (Rome). This was the ultimate move in an act of seer desperation played out on the chessboard of the history of the eastern portion of the Roman Byzantine Empire. After all, it was the ecclesiastical authority of the emperors that held the East and West together. The move of the Seat of Christianity from the East (Africa) to the West (Europe) was imminent. Two attempts to call a crusade were unsuccessful.

John was met with bitter opposition when he returned to Constantinople. The people of Constantinople rejected the union agreement, and they refused to submit to the West. In the meantime, the threat of the Turks did not diminish and military assistance from the West to save Constantinople was not forthcoming. The Council remained seated until 1445, which was the same year that the building of St. Peters Church in Rome commenced. The West had achieved its goals. John conceded on long standing issues. He agreed that the Latins could use the filioque (son) in the creed, eat unleavened bread at Mass without danger to faith or right customs, and he accepted western supremacy over the Patriarch of the Hagia Sophia. Perhaps, the chief result of the Council was the passing of the ecclesiastical authority from the Emperors to the West. The Emperor would no longer hold the office of Vicar of Christ. The Vicar of Christ would sit in Europe. (Today, the Pope in the Vatican is considered the Vicar of Christ).

John VIII, unfortunately, learned very little from the history of deception by the West as his predecessors experienced or from the previous roguish crusades from the West. There was no turning back, only delay. He would remain in office until 1448. What his fate was is unclear. His brother, Constantine XI, succeeded him as Emperor.

Constantine continued in vain to try to secure military assistance from the West. In 1451, the Turks built a Castle on the Bosporus, clearly sending a signal that it was a matter of time before they would siege Constantinople. Still striving to survive, the Act of Union, the joining of the East and West, was proclaimed in 1452 by the Emperor in the Hagia Sophia. The people of Constantinople agreed to the union. However, it proved to be futile. The West had the much-coveted ecclesiastical authority. There was no incentive to provide military assistance. The Turks were advancing. The East would cease to be a source of contention once the Turks completed the decimation of the Byzantine Empire.

In May 1453, Sultan Muhammed II seized one of the most heavily fortified cities in the world, Constantinople, the capital of the Byzantine Empire. The Ottoman Turks and their ruler Sultan Muhammed II led the successful attack. Muhammed achieved his long-standing goal to seize Constantinople and end the strong hold of the Byzantine Empire in Constantinople. It was estimated that approximately 10,000 men defended the city to no avail. The Turk's infantry was estimated to be between 100,000 and 150,000. The Turks employed the latest war methods and tactics. Cannons were used to blowholes in the walls of the double walled city of Constantinople in order to enter and take control. Warships cut the city's sea defense. Constantine's army and sea defense were no match for the Turks. With approximately 8000 men including some from the West Constantine fought for two months until he died in battle defending his empire. Constantine XI would be the last of the Byzantine Emperors. Constantinople had fallen.

The city that Sultan Mahomet II or Muhammed II had wanted for the capital of the Ottoman Empire was now his although it was greatly diminished. The capture of Constantinople gave the Ottoman Sultan an opportunity to follow the lead of the Ptolomies and other Byzantine Emperors who came before him. Monophysites turned Muhammedans living under the Ottoman Turkish rule and government would merge once again in the Ottoman Empire just as Dyophysitic Christianity and State interconnected during the Byzantine Empire.

The usurping wars and greed for riches, political, and religious authority finally took their toll. For over nine

What Happened to the Church of Hagia Sophia?

hundred years Constantinople was the capital of Christian Civilization and the Christian world, and the Church of Hagia Sophia was at the center of state, religious life, and all the pageantry of the Roman Byzantine Empire. The Turkish conquest marked the end of the Church's reign as the first Seat (See) of Christianity, the first University and learning institution for Europeans, and the beginning of the world's prototype for Mosques. In spite of all the earthquakes and conflicts, the Church of Hagia Sophia physically survived.

The building with its last remaining artifacts remained essentially undisturbed. Sultan Muhammed II converted the Church of Hagia Sophia or Aya Sofya (in Arabic) into a mosque in 1453. He added so-called Arabic characters characterizing the building as a mosque. It would remain a mosque for the Muhammedans until 1919. The first minaret was added during the reign of the Ottoman Sultan Bayezid II (1481-1512) then two more were added during the reign of the Ottoman Sultan Selim II (1566-1574) and the fourth and last was added during the reign of the Ottoman Sultan Murad III (1574-1595).

Note: The minaret is taken from the building designs of the African Melchite Spanish Moors who created, designed, and built the cities of Granada, Cordoba, Seville, in Spain and other areas beginning in 1051. Thus bringing a high civilization to the Europeans of Spain. Their architecture not only can be seen in the Hagia Sophia, but also can be seen in the design of the Cathedral of St. Basil in Moscow, Russia and the design of the Taj Mahal in Agra, India.

Hagia Sophia not only continued to serve as the prototype for all future Mosques and Churches throughout the world, it also served as a model for State Capitol buildings. The dome remains a prevalent architectural feature among Church and Government buildings. Aya Sophia or St. Sophia remained a Mosque throughout the duration of the Ottoman Empire for almost 500 years, until World War I when the British toppled the Ottoman-Turkish Empire in 1918-1919. The League of Nations mandated Turkey to the British.

After almost 1400 years of virtually uninterrupted use as a place of worship by at least two faiths, some say three faiths, the Great Church of Hagia Sophia or in Turkish, Aya Sophia, came to an end as a place of worship. Aya Sophia would become a museum after Mustafa Kemal Ataturk, a Macedonian, came to power. His goal was to westernize Turkey. Ataturk was a man who understood the East and the West for he had grown up where the two mingled. His tactic was to change the culture and customs of the people of Turkey. He began by first removing the white wash that covered the original Christian mosaic artwork. Once the clean up was done, he began to convert it to a Byzantine-Ottoman Art Museum in 1934. It continues to stand today in modern Istanbul, Turkey, where its treasures and splendor remain legendary.

I will conclude similarly to how I began my

introduction to this chapter. Again, it is astonishing that the Great Church /Mosque stands today in Istanbul, Turkey with all its glory and history unknown by the majority of the populous or religious believers of the world and rarely discussed if any by the theologians or the western academic community. Albeit, after all is said and done, this was an edifice that was dedicated to and housed mythology. For this was the building where the created creature, Christ, was worshiped for over 900 years and where the first created god, Muhammed, for the Muhammedans was worshiped during the time of the Ottoman Turks (1453-1919).

Hagia Sophia continues in 2003 to be the pride and joy and the premier tourist attraction of Istanbul, Turkey. Interestingly, Istanbul is presented to the world today as the only city in the world in which mosques and churches have coexisted for centuries.

Under Mustafa Kemal Ataturk, Ankara replaced Istanbul as the capital of Turkey in 1923. This represented the complete disestablishment of the Ottoman Empire, signifying the end of Aya Sophia as a mosque and the abolition of the Sultanate. A New Turkish Republic was established. Religion ceased to be a political instrument and became a matter of individual conscience. Religion and State separated in Turkey. The long-standing symbol of conflict and unity between the East and West was slated to become a Museum. Hagia Sophia or Aya Sofya was placed under the auspices of the Minister of

Byzantine Institute in America began restoration of Hagia Sophia in 1932. It was opened as a museum in 1934 without religious affiliation and is hailed as one of the outstanding monuments of Turkey. Aya Sofya is open to the public.

Arnetta Williams
Society of New Scholars (SUNS)
Chicago, Illinois

A note to the Christians, Muslims, and Jews: "Religious Mythology has been and continues to be at the root of most conflicts and wars. Our natural human spirituality is what connects us one to another. Let's consciously connect and make peace."

SUMMARY

It has been said that belief has a quality of its own, but fact can destroy misguided belief. Especially, for those who can view the evidence with an open mind.

Walter Williams, through countless years of study and research has penetrated the veil that has held religion a mystery. Starting with *The Historical Origin of Christianity*, he has uncovered through research that Muhammadenism (Moslem)/Islam is only a derivative of Christianity via Monophysite Christianity and a subsequent Monist ideology along with its numerous modifications over time to its final conclusion. This fact has been hidden from the world at large, outside of the Muhammadenism/Islam world.

Walter Williams has simply confined himself to what he believes to be the facts. And hopes that the contents of this book will be of interest to those persons who are anxious to impartially investigate the subject. Walter Williams, traces the puzzle from Monophysite Christianity through 921 years of Byzantine history before the time of Muhiyuddin Ibn Al 'Arabi. Muhiyuddin Ibn Al'Arabi's biography and life were used to create the created creature, the Prophet Muhammad, for traditional Islam. Ibn Al' Arabi is credited also with the development of the pilgrimage of the Hajj ritual. He wrote a systematic treatise on religious matters. And used this system to put his dreams, wanderings, illusions, musings, and visions in writings. No systematic study of the writings of Muhiyuddin Ibn Al' Arabi was attempted until the 1930's.

The writings of Muhiyuddin Ibn Al' Arabi are the least known to the modern world. Without the use of his life and biography, Islam as we view it today would be very different.

Walter Williams has unraveled the tumultuous threads of The Historical Origin of Muhammadenism/Islam, and many other areas connected to its history. To fully understand any history, one must endeavor to understand what preceded it, and to fully analyze how it in fact came about. Traditional stories that have been embellished and elaborated on for centuries cannot stand in the light of assured facts. Such as the chapters on: The Coming of Europeans to Africa, The Foundation for the Creation of the Name Muhammad, Monophysite/Dyophysitic Christians, The Council of Nicaea II-Image Making Versus Iconoclasm, Crusades in Africa, Comments and Questions About Mecca and Medina Outside of Islamic Tradition, Who Was Shaikh Al 'Akbar Muhiyuddin Ibn Al a.k.a., Ibn 'Arabi, alias Muhammad?, The Decline of Muhammadenism and the Rise of Islam, Things to Think About Outside of Islamic Tradition, What Happened to the Hagia Sophia?, and The Connection Between Christianity and Islam. It is hoped that the reader will not only read the aforementioned chapters, but to study them for understanding. Because, when one puts his or her natural divine spiritual destiny in the hands of another,

what happens when that path runs out? Please, remember that the history of religion is only the history of symbolism. When symbolism is presented as a story, it becomes myth.

In conclusion, it has been said that: A great deal of intelligence can be turned into ignorance when the need for illusion runs deep. This need for illusion reminds me of a quantum singularity (a black hole in space). But, in this instant the black hole is in the realm of the so-called Three Great Religions. And Muhammadenism/Islam is the one in question at this time although this question could equally apply to all three religions. Each and every one of us was born with free will. And it is hoped that each of us will use that free will along with truth and knowledge instead of mere traditions to direct our Creator given natural divine spiritual destiny.

Robert D. Sommerville
Society of New Scholars (SUNS)
Chicago, Illinois

CONCLUDING COMMENTS

In this book I have taken you on a journey through history, revealing to you a history that evolved from real people, time, places, and events. This book is written to set your spirit free from all religious bondage. Religion and religious literature are tools that western society uses under its control to indoctrinate the world masses. Always remember Carter G. Woodson, the great educator and author of *The Mis-Education of the Negro*, who said, "If you can control a man's thinking you do not have to worry about his actions. If he has been trained to go to the back door and upon arriving at the back he find no door, he then will make a back door." Since we as a people of African descent have been spiritually disconnected from our Ancient Egyptian ancestors, and other African ancient cultures, we do not think and live our lives as subjects of our own ancestral historical experience. Therefore, we conduct our lives based on false illusions and mythology via the Bible/Koran and other religious written literature. This is set in place for us by the European society through their educational and religious network systems.

European institutions are used as vehicles of mass mind control, which rely on the news media to do their part in this farce. Now I am going to give you a fact to think about, Jewish writings are in both Christianity and Islam via The Old Testament for the Christians and The Pentateuch and Psalms are in Islam via the Koran. Conversely, neither Christian or Islamic writings are anywhere to be found in Jewish literature. I am referring to the religious literature that is used in their synagogues such as their Sefer ha Torah and Mishna Talmud. It is not by accident that this was done. It was done on purpose and by design with cunning and political intent.

I now quote Joshua Armstrong from his book entitled The Seekers; "The best way to develop the mind is cultivating the spirit. Regrettably, many people turn to organized religion for the care and feeding of their spiritual lives when in fact organized religions is often more interested in emotionalism than spirituality. Going to Church on Sunday can be like being in a bar fight where fists are flying, glass is breaking, and bodies are falling. With all the singing, preaching, and hallelujah, the service becomes a blinding emotional whirlwind. The spirit is a delicate plant. It cannot thrive under the tumultuous conditions presented in that kind of church service. Myths, parables, swelling music, testimonials, and hysteria-none of this help the spirit develop. True spirituality comes through lessons that are applicable to every day life. This was the way Ancient Egyptian spirituality was taught through the here and now. The chores and choices that we have before us in this world not through fantastic tales of what will be in a place no living person has ever seen. The answers we seek are not inside a church or on an altar or on the lips of a preacher. They are within us. If through the pursuit of the spirit, we can connect with our own minds, the answers will be there. We will choose our own destinies. We will not be subject to random influences. We will have our minds and never lose them." Another Armstrong quote: "Church doors are always open to whoever wants to enter, but they are open to those who are willing to be sheep. The service of God is really service to those self-proclaimed holy men who hold the franchise. Accumulating material grandeur is the goal, not the improvement of the people's lives. Independent thought is discouraged. Raising the individual up is not part of the plan; keeping the flock docile, distracted, and deluded is what it's all about." If you the reader can understand these quotes, you are now on your way to removing the shackles of all religions and religious literature that have been clogging your spiritual connection with the universe. Further, this spiritual connection that you have with the Higher Power of Creation and the universe was given to you at the time of your birth. You must find your way back to your own in-dwelling spirituality. And in so doing, you will never have to seek or have the need for religion or god. All religions come packaged with a God and religious literature. Christianity is packaged, for example, with a dead Caucasian man on a cross, the created creature called Jesus the Christ as god and saviour along with Christian and Jewish writings called the Old Testament and Christian writings called the New Testament. On the other hand, Islam comes packaged with a faceless white male image-icon riding on a camel called the Prophet Muhammed along with the Koran, which contains Jewish writings (The Pentateuch and

Psalms) and Christian writings (The four gospels) along with Allah as "The God."

The man created religion called Judaism also comes packaged with its created characters such as Abraham, Isaac, Jacob, Moses, and the list of names can go on and on. Remember Judaism is not a B.C. religion. Judaism as a religion began with Solomon bar Isaac, called RASHI, starting in 1080-1100. It continued through the ages with other Jewish Tosafot appendix writers such as the grandson of RASHI, Jacob Ben Meir, Moses Maimon called Maimonides, and a whole group of unknown Jewish scholars, Rabbis, and non-Jewish scholars with all creating and writing their own Pirke Avot through the centuries. This religion also comes with its created god called Jehovah or Yahweh.

At this point I want to reiterate what my wife, Arnetta, told me about God one day. She said, "God is an abstract idea that needs human spirituality to give it life." Always remember that god is a term that can be used only in and for religion:

1. God is a man created by man and in man's own image and not the reverse. Note: When the name god is used and spoken of by human beings, the pronouns are masculine, he, his, or him, which refer to a man or male figure.

2. God as a man cannot create or bring forth anything

with life in it singularly. God as man has to be mated with a Goddess, the female, in order to bring forth pro-life.

3. God can only exist if you the human being give these various religious gods life by giving these gods your spiritual power that was given to you by the Creator/Creatress at the time of your birth. This is done by the human being believing and placing personal faith in non-living religious, man-created gods.

4. If you the human being took god, Jesus the Christ, Allah, Jehovah, Jahw'h, Buddha, or any other religious gods that are connected to a religion and discarded them along with the Bible, Koran, Sefer Ha Torah/Talmud, or any other religious literature. What would be left? Standing would be you with your alive spirit that your Creator/Creatress gave you at inception. Knowing this should tell you that your spiritual power that dwells inside of you gives these man-created words and religious named characters Life. Without your spiritual power, these religious gods and religious literature (Bible, Koran, and Torah/Talmud) would be dead.

5. Warning: Do not believe in God. Why not? (A) Because this robs you of your in-dwelling spiritual power that is connected to the cosmic mind of the

universe. (B) Believing in God encourages you to come outside of yourself and give your spiritual power to a dead man made god and a dead man hanging on a cross, therefore, robing one's self of your own divine birth right which is your in-dwelling spirit.

Note: The author of this book realizes and knows that there is a higher power than himself. What it is I do not know, but what I do know is that this higher power has created everything that your eyes can see in the physical realm. That includes me the author, therefore, do not think of the author of this book as an atheist.

I have written this book to set you spiritually free of all religious bondage that our Melchite Coptic Egyptian ancestors unwittingly helped to set into motion (Christianity/Islam). Western society uses these religions as political tools to impose on and indoctrinate the world masses. Many times after giving a lecture on the historical origin of Christianity, Islam, and Judaism, I am asked a question. "If what you say is true and there never have been men that walked the earth in human form of any race, creed, or color by the names of Jesus the Christ, Muhammed the Prophet, Abraham, Isaac, and Jacob, or Moses, then what do I put in its place?"

My answer to the above question is you were not born with a religion. Religion was imposed upon you and introduced to you at an early and innocent age in your life. Always remember you were born with a divine spiritual birthright and that divine in-dwelling spiritual birthright was given to you at the time of your birth by the Higher Power of Creation who used your mother and father as human instruments to bring you forth in human form. Thus giving you a divine spiritual birthright, which is your life spirit that dwells inside of you at this very moment. At the time of your birth, your divine in-dwelling spirit or spirituality was connected to and spiritually in tune with the spiritual consciousness and rhythm of the universe. You are connected to the universe through your pineal gland that's connected to your brain fibers, which are connected to your nostrils, taking in the air that you breathe. The pineal gland serves as a conduit between you and your universe. Thereby, you received the spiritual power to sustain yourself as long as you live. The air that you breathe keeps you in spiritual consciousness with your Creator/Creatress and the spiritual rhythm of the universe, giving you a personal relationship with the Creator/Creatress or Higher Power of Creation.

I have been fortunate to escape the influence of any man-made religion and not allow any god to sever or confuse my personal relation with the universe and my Creator/Creatress. You were born with the same birthright. Use it. Always remember that you were born spiritually free of all man-made religions. No human being was born with a religion. By not understanding your natural spiritual connection with the universe and your Creator/Creatress, many have allowed man to confuse and substitute their naturally given spiritual birthright with one of his man-made unnatural religions. This is similar to being introduced to cigarettes, alcohol, or drugs. You, the human being, did not come into this world smoking cigarettes, using alcohol, drugs, or religion. These unnatural habits are all man introduced. Always remember that our African ancestors the Ancient Egyptians and other Africans living throughout the continent of Africa never had or practiced a religion during the time of antiquity. They had a spiritual way of life that was in tune with the cosmic laws of the universe. They were students of the universe. Therefore, I urge you to become a student of the universe just like your Ancient Egyptian African and other African ancestors who lived throughout the continent of Africa. (See Chapter I). At this point, I must warn you about the religious custom of "praying." Religion encourages one to pray to a man created god for their needs, substance, wants, and desires. When this is done, it puts human beings in a position of begging for their substance because praying is a form of begging. If you understand your spiritual connection and spiritual power connected to and coming from the universe via your pineal gland, you will then realize how praying is a waste of your human spiritual energy. Your needs, wants, and desires can be manifested first in spiritual form and then in physical form just for the asking. This is done when the human being makes up her or his mind regarding what they want from the universe. When this is decided, you will receive instructions from the universe on how to go about manifesting your thoughts into reality. Listening to that little voice from within and following your intuition, hunches, or ideas will achieve this. After all this is your spiritual birthright.

The introduction of religion was done to place governments, nations, and the entire civilized world under the control of an assortment of man-organized religions or ways of thinking. One must remember that all religions today are used as political tools of control. Political, military, economic (including taxation), and social control have proven to be easier under man-made religious rulership. This was also the smoothest path for eventual world domination and the acquisition of absolute power, misdistribution of wealth, and a world population of obedient religious slaves. I now conclude by sharing with you what I was told many years ago about the word, "facts." Facts, I was told, are "stronger than argument, more profound than reasoning, more dependable than opinions, silence dispute, supercede predictions, and facts always end the argument. I have done my duty by putting the facts in writing. Now you must judge for yourself.

Walter Williams
Historian and Research Analyst of Ancient History
Founder: The Ancient Egyptian Museum
    The Ancient Egyptian Institute
    The Ancient Egyptian Research Society
    Society of New Scholars (SUNS), Chicago, IL

P.S. I hope you, the reader, will take the information

written in this book to liberate yourself from all religious bondage. And, find your way back to your own personal in-dwelling spiritual power and connection that you have with the universe. It is my earnest hope that the repetition in this book has helped you to better follow and understand the message and some of the historical events that evolved throughout history.

Ma'at Hotep,

(Love and Peace)

W.W.

GLOSSARY OF TERMS

A.B.C.E. – The term A.B.C.E. (or After B.C.E.) is used by the author to denote the time when B.C.E. ended, and includes the time until the close of the Council of Chalcedon (451 A.B.C.E.). At this point, the Christian Era officially began; therefore, A.C.E. or (After the Christian Era) can then be historically correct, the term After B.C.E. was invented by the author.

COPTIC CHRISTIAN - A Coptic Egyptian who accepted the Dyophysitic union or two natures of Serapis/Christ at the Council of Ephesus in 431.

COPTIC EGYPTIAN - A direct descendant of the Ancient Egyptians.

DHIMMI – The protected status afforded to non-Muslim communities in a Muhammedan or Islamic State, whereby, such communities are guaranteed the right to practice religious, administrative, and political freedom with the payment of a reasonable tax.

DYOPHISITIC – Divine spirit and human nature combining both into one. The Coptics who accepted this union at the Council of Ephesus were called Christians.

HADITH – In tradition, a record of actions and or sayings attributed to the Prophet Muhammed and his companions.

HAJJ – The pilgrimage to an imaginary Mecca or a physical journey. The fifth pillar of traditional Islam.

MONIST/MONISM - Belief in one substance. In metaphysics, a term applied to that type of theory that seeks to explain the universe with all its phenomena by a single principle, thus reducing the whole of reality to unity. In seeking to explain the apparent contradictions in a world where mind seems to be distinct from matter and soul seems distinct from body, monist theories differ considerably in the choice of the principle, which is made the basis of unification. It may be material. If substance and energy of a physical nature are regarded as the only reality, or it may be spiritual. If mind or spirit is taken as the reality by which all is to be explained, the resulting systems then will represent materialistic or naturalistic or idealistic or spiritualistic monism. An ultimate principle may be adopted in which the opposites are shown to be held in equipoise or equal balance. Monism stands in opposition to dualism and pluralism.

> Note: Shaikh Al Akbar Muhiyuddin Ibn Al' Arabi alias Muhammed was a monist. He saw the world through Monism, especially when it involved religion. His Monist ideology is used today as the underlying principle in the religion of Muhammed or Islam as evidenced by the cry of the Muslims, "There is only one God."

MONOPHYSITISM - The position that Serapis/Christ has no human nature, only an Osiris assimilated spirit.

SHARIA - In the teachings of traditional Islam, Sharia is the way or the divine path of true obedience to God, the large body of legal tradition, which informs the community about the nature of the faithfulness that God requires of it.

SHE/HE CREATOR/CREATRESS - A term used by the author to recognize the universe as being female and male, thus giving cosmic balance.

SUFI (Tasawwuf) - From the root 'suf'' meaning wool to denote the wearing of a woolen robe by those who have devoted themselves to the mystic life and becoming a Sufi.

TARIKA - A term meaning "roadway, path" in Islamic mysticism.

BIBLIOGRAPHY

1. Abdalati, Hammudah, Islam in Focus, American Trust Publications, Indianapolis, IN, 1975

2. Ali, Ameer, A Short History of the Saracens, MacMillan and Company, London, 1889, 1951.

3. Al-Qabesi, Muhyiddin, Collector and Editor of The Holy Quran and The Sword, Saudi Desert House Publishing and Distribution, 1998.

4. An-Nawawis, Forty Hadith, Saudi Desert House Publishing and Distribution, 1998.

5. Armstrong, Joshua and Bruno, Anthony, The Seekers, Harper Collins Publishers, 2000.

6. Austin, R.W.J., Ibn Al'Arabi, The Bezels of Wisdom, Paulist. Press, Inc., Mahwah, New Jersey 1980.

7. Berry, Gerald L., Religions of the World, Barnes and Noble, Inc., 1947.

8. Bullet, Richard W., Islam: The View From the Edge, Columbia University Press, New York, NY, 1994.

9. Chaitanya, Krishna, A History of Arabic Literature,

Ramesh Jain, Manohar Publications, New Delhi, India, 1983.

10. Cragg, Kenneth, The Call of the Minaret, Oxford University Press, Inc., 1956. A Galaxy Book, New York Oxford University Press, 1964.

11. Crone, Patricia, Meccan Trade and The Rise of Islam, Princeton University Press, 1987.

12. Cutler, H.G. and Yaggy, M.S., Panorama of Nations, J.V.F. Company, Chicago, IL, 1892.

13. Gibb, H.A.R. and Krause, J.H., Shorter Encyclopedia of Islam, Cornell University Press, Ithaca, New York, 1953

14. Gibb, H.A.R., Muhammedanism, Mentor Books by arrangement with Oxford University Press, Inc., New York, 1955.

15. Gibb, H.A.R., The Meaning of the Glorious Koran, Mentor Books by Arrangement with George Allen and Unwin, LTD., 1953. New York, New York.

16. Haines, Byron L. and Cooley, Frank L., Christians

and Muslims Together, The Geneva Press, Philadelphia, PA, 1987.

17. Holmes, William Gordon, The Age of Justinian and Theodora, George Bell and Sons Publishers, London, 1905.

18. Itzkowitz, Norman, Ottoman Empire and Islamic Tradition, University of Chicago, IL, 1972.

19. Jenkins, Romilly, Byzantium: The Imperial Centuries AD 610-1071, University of Toronto Press, Toronto, Canada, 1995.

20. Khan, Khaja, Studies in Tasawwuf, S.H. Muhammed Ashraf Publishers, Booksellers and exporters, Taibak

21. Road, New Anarkali, Lahore – 7 Pakistan. Reprinted 1990.

22. Kinross, Lord and the editors of the Newsweek Book Division, Hagia Sophia, Newsweek, New York,1972.

23. Kinross, Lord, The Ottoman Centuries, Morrow Quill Paperbacks, New York, 1977.

24. Knysh, Alexander, D., Ibn Arabi in the Later Islamic Traditional, State University of New York Press, 1999.

25. Lamb, Harold, The Crusades, Doubleday, Doran and Company, Inc., 1930.

26. Lewis, Bernard, The Arabs in History, Harper Torch Books, Harper and Row, 1960.

27. Mainstone, Rowland J., Hagia Sophia, Thames and Hudson, Inc, New York, 1988.

28. Nazir-Ali, Michael, Islam: A Christian Perspective, The Westminster Press, Philadelphia, PA, 1983.

29. Nicholson, Reynolds A, Studies in Islamic Mysticism, reprinted by Curzon Press LTD, Richmond, England, 1994. First published by Cambridge University Press, 1921.

30. Smith, Houston, The Religious of Man, Harper and Row Publishers, Inc., New York, New York, 1958.

31. Stewart, Desmond and the Editors of Time-Life Books, Early Islam, Time-Life Books, New York.

32. Thalheimer, M.F., an outline of General History, Van Antwerp, Bragg and Company, Cincinnati, Ohio 1877.

33. Watt, William Montgomery, Early Islam Collected

Articles, Edinburgh University Press, 1990.

34. Williams, Walter, The Historical Origin of
    Christianity, Maathian Press, Inc., Chicago, IL, 1993.

35. Columbia Encyclopedia, Volume I, second edition,
    edited by William Bridgewater and Elizabeth J.
    Sherwood, Columbia University Press, Morningside
    Heights, New York, 1950.

36. Encyclopedia Dictionary of Judaica, Edited by
    Geoffrey Wigoder, Keter Publishing House
    Jerusalem, LTD, 1974.

37. Woodson, Carter G., The Mis-Education of the
    Negro, African World Press, Inc., P.O. Box 1892,
    Trenton, NJ 08618.

38. World Book Encyclopedia, Field Enterprises
    Educational Corporation, 1974.

TO

CONTACT THE AUTHOR

FOR

LECTURES, RADIO/ TELEVISION INTERVIEW

e-mail: ancientegyptian@msn.com